Cannabis Cupcakes

Cannabis Cupcakes

35 mini marijuana cakes to bake and decorate

CHRIS STONE & CAROL ANN

TEN SPEED PRESS
Berkeley

Text and illustrations copyright © 2013 by
Elephant Book Company Limited

Published in the United States by Ten Speed Press,
an imprint of the Crown Publishing Group,
a division of Random House, Inc., New York,
by arrangement with Elephant Book Company Limited,
35 Fournier Street, London E1 6QE, United Kingdom

www.crownpublishing.com
www.tenspeed.com

Ten Speed Press and the Ten Speed colophon
are registered trademarks of
Random House, Inc.

Editorial Director: Will Steeds
Project Editor: Lewis Esson
Cover and Interior Design: Lindsey Johns
Illustrations: Watchbell
Copy Editor: Kristi Hein

Ten Speed Press Editor: Lisa Westmoreland

Library of Congress Cataloging-in-Publication Data
is on file with the publisher.

ISBN 978-1-60774-386-6

Printed in China

10 9 8 7 6 5 4 3 2 1

First Edition

Contents

Introduction

Cupcakes made their first appearance in the nineteenth century. It's not entirely clear why they were called "cupcakes," but some food historians think it may simply be because the cakes were originally cooked in cups that would stand the heat of the oven, or possibly because the ingredients used to make them were measured out by means of cups.

Why cupcakes?

Cupcakes had the advantage of cooking much more quickly than larger cakes and, of course, each made a perfect individual serving without the messy business of slicing larger cakes. Muffin pans (also called "gem pans") were popular at the beginning of the twentieth century, so people also started to make cupcakes in small pans. In the last few years, cupcakes have become an amazingly

popular trend in the culinary world, and there are numerous bakeries devoted entirely to them. These little treats have really caught the imagination of the public as they are comparatively easy to bake, decorate, and personalize—even for stoners—and make great party treats. Along with the timeless classic recipes such as vanilla and chocolate, there's now a huge variety of cupcakes in every flavor under the sun. As far as decorations go, the sky's the limit.

Psychedelic Fresh Cherry Cupcakes (pages 62–63).

So where's the appeal here for potheads? Well, you might still be a slave to your rolling mat and bong, but plenty of other stoners around the world are getting high in the kitchen. Yes, baking's de rigueur these days. Simply, you're not rollin' with it if you ain't got a rolling pin. The daintyness of the cupcakes might seem girly but they're a great size for a quick hit—think of it like a quick toot on your pipe. And the sweet and indulgent toppings are perfect for disguising the taste of cannabis, which even the most diehard enthusiast would have to concede is pretty rank. You'll find lots of creative ideas in this book—cupcakes with a toker's twist from the addition of that unique ingredient!

Cupcakes are great served up with a cup of coffee and a cheeky reefer, dressed up with fruit and ice cream as a dessert, or as a colorful centerpiece for a celebration or special occasion. The thirty-five cupcake recipes in this book use Souped-Up Sunflower Oil and Boosted Butter (see pages 12–17), both especially good in sweet recipes. The cupcakes are best eaten fresh to enjoy them at their best—either the day you make them or the day after.

Some Cupcake Basics

1) **Greasing Cupcake Pans**: Brush the inside of the baking pan with oil or melted butter, using a pastry brush, or use a piece of wax paper to rub a dab of butter around the pan. This stops the food from sticking to the pan. If you're using paper cups to line the pans, there's no need to grease the pans.

2) **In the Oven**: Always ensure you preheat the oven—it will take around 15 minutes to reach the temperature needed before baking. Ovens do vary and cooking times will vary with different ovens, so the baking time is a guide. However much you're craving some sweet Mary Jane, resist the temptation to open the oven door before the cake batter has set. Wait to check if the cakes are cooked after the minimum baking time; a sudden whoosh of cold air can cause the cakes to sink before they've had time to set.

3) **Out of the Oven:** The golden rule is to let the cupcakes sit undisturbed for at least 5–10 minutes after they come out of the oven, as their insides go on cooking due

Chocolate, Pecan, and Marshmallow Cupcake (pages 40–42).

to residual heat. After this initial period, they need to be left to cool on a wire rack (an oven or broiler rack makes a perfect stand-in) so they will now cool down more rapidly and uniformly.

For advice on any specialist equipment you will need, see pages 18–19.

Happy baking!

chapter **1**

CANCAKE BASICS

Baking isn't difficult if you put your (feeble) mind to it, but you need to know some basics before you start. Let's face it, everyone needs to begin somewhere and these cupcakes won't make themselves. So, settle down with a coffee and a big fat j and prepare to get a culinary brain dump on, among other things, preparing your pot, getting the all-important dosage levels correct, and familiarizing yourself with some common kitchen tools.

Why Eat Your Weed?

So which is better: smoking a fat j or eating a cannabis cupcake? Sure, the smoke is more sharable, but when you assess the pros and cons of smoking weed versus ingesting it, cannabis cooking wins out every time.
Here are the factors to consider:

Health considerations—Cannabis itself is not carcinogenic, but the plant material often contains many impurities (depending on its provenance) that, when burned and inhaled, can cause major health issues over time. And if you roll your weed with tobacco—well, we don't have to tell you how toxic and highly addictive tobacco is, do we? In contrast, there are no health risks associated with eating properly cooked ganja. In fact, cannabis is a nutritious fiber and its seed a source of edible oil.

Discretion—There's no mistaking the distinctive smell of burning cannabis, and though you may love the smell, there are many other noses that disapprove (especially those of the feds). But eating an innocent hash cupcake will arouse no suspicion whatsoever—as long as you control the hysterical giggling and uninhibited body language.

The high—The active ingredients in weed (the parts that get you wasted) are called "cannabinoids." The most pertinent of these is delta 9-tetrahydrocannabinol ("THC" to you and me). THC is more effective if combined with fats—the fat molecules link onto the THC molecules so they are more efficiently absorbed into your bloodstream and thence by your brain, where all the fun starts.

So if you prepare your cannabis cupcakes correctly, you'll get a more intense, cerebral, and longer-lasting high than the buzz from a couple of bong hits. Many ganja gourmets have likened the buzz to an LSD trip, so you need to experiment and fine-tune your dosage levels. (See Get Dosed! on page 17.) However, once you've figured out the amount that works for you in a favorite recipe, you have more control of the precise dosage to use—as long as you have a source with consistent potency.

Taste—Some cannabis aficionados love the distinctive redolence of the smoke; others would prefer the high without it. If you're one of those, you'll love the way ganja cupcakes override any leafy flavor with the sweet, spicy, nutty, and creamy qualities everyone loves in a sweet treat. As you'll learn in Easy Oven-Ready Pot (see pages 12–15), there are two effective methods for "distilling" out the grassiness while concentrating the active ingredients.

Economy—Obviously, when you smoke a joint most of the good stuff literally goes up in smoke between tokes and doesn't make it to your lungs (and bloodstream) where it would take effect. Smoking grass is also wasteful in that only the buds are smoked; the leaves, stalks, and seeds are thrown away (unless you're feeling thrifty or desperate). But when you use grass in food, you can use every part of the plant. The process of making Boosted Butter

(see page 12) or Souped-Up Sunflower Oil (see page 15) breaks down these "discards," and you get the benefit of all the active compounds.

Pain relief—For people suffering from chronic illnesses like multiple sclerosis and arthritis, cooked cannabis provides pain relief without the addiction and side effects associated with narcotic pain relievers. And the relief you get from eating it lasts longer.

Finally, baking is just way more creatively satisfying than packing a bong or rolling a doobie. Just wait 'til you see the look on your friends' faces when you bring out a tray of Almond Pirate Cupcakes or Magic Bus Red Velvet Cupcakes.

Waiting for the Hit

We need to point out one key difference between smoking weed and ingesting it (though it is certainly not a negative)—that is, the timing and the duration of its effect. When you inhale smoke, the THC reaches your bloodstream quickly; the hit is more or less instantaneous and the high may last an hour before wearing off. When you eat cannabis, it must be digested (via your gut) along with what it's cooked or baked in, so it will take time to reach your bloodstream—as much as two hours—and the effects may last as long as eight hours.

With this in mind, err on the side of caution: if you're planning on a dedicated cannabis cupcake session, take the rest of the day off.

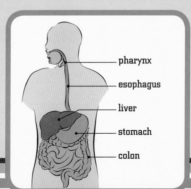

- pharynx
- esophagus
- liver
- stomach
- colon

Easy Oven-Ready Pot

There are two main ways that you can choose to incorporate your stash into the cupcake recipes that follow—cannabis-infused butter or oil. The infused butter and "augmented" oil do require advance preparation before you start turning out actual cupcakes, but both methods will leave you well stocked for multiple baking sessions.

How to Make Boosted Butter

I Using a blender or coffee grinder, grind your stash into a very fine powder.

Boosted Butter is the best way to introduce the goodness from your chronic into any recipe. It can be stored (refrigerated or frozen) for months without spoiling.

2 ounces (55 g) high-quality
  bud, hash, or leaf

2 cups (455 g) butter

MONEY-SAVING TIPS

Two ounces may sound like a lot of weed to lay your hands on. And the cost of acquiring it may be prohibitive. However, considering that most smokers have no use for cannabis leaves, most growers will happily give you a few bags for free. If that's not an option, just scale down your pot-to-butter ratio accordingly—for example, 1/2 ounce (14 g) of weed and 1/2 cup (1/4 pound/113g) of butter.

WASTE NOT, WANT NOT

Leftover leafy material from the process of making Boosted Butter can be simmered in hot milk or vodka to make a tasty and potent drink.

2 In a large, heavy saucepan, bring about 3 cups (720 ml) water to a boil.

3 Add the butter and ground cannabis to the boiling water. When the butter has melted, reduce the heat to low, cover the pan, and simmer for approximately 2 hours, stirring occasionally. Turn off the heat and let the solution rest for 2 to 3 minutes.

4 Strain the cannabis-rich liquid butter through a sieve or cheese-cloth into a separate container to remove any unwanted particles. Any debris that remains can be discarded or consumed separately (see box).

5 Let the liquid butter cool completely, then cover the bowl and place in the refrigerator overnight to separate.

6 In the morning you will see that a deep layer of hardened butter has formed at the top of the bowl. Discard the liquid that remains. (Don't drink it!)

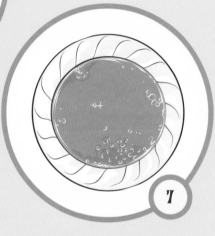

7 Keep the butter refrigerated (or ideally frozen) to ensure that it does not go bad. You now have a supply of butter that can be substituted for normal fat in any recipe. You can even spread it on toast!

WEED OR HASH?

While the "budding" cannabis baker can use any part of the marijuana plant for cooking, hashish (as long as it's of high quality) is the best choice, because much of the preparation has already taken place during its manufacture (in which bud is repeatedly strained and compressed to turn it into hash) and it dissolves well in fat.

How to Make Souped-Up Sunflower Oil

The advantage of Souped-Up Sunflower Oil is that you can store it for a long time at ordinary room temperature without its going bad. Sunflower oil has a high smoke point (that is, the maximum temperature to which you can heat an oil before it becomes unhealthy to eat), which makes it ideal for baking. Sunflower oil is also a very healthy cooking oil, composed of 79 percent monounsaturated fat, 7 percent polyunsaturated fat, and only 14 percent saturated fat—almost the same composition as extra-virgin olive oil. It does, however, have the distinct advantage in cupcake baking of not having as strong a flavor as olive oil.

2 cups (480 ml) sunflower oil

2 ounces (55 g) grass or hash

COVERT OPS

Using Boosted Butter or Souped-Up Sunflower Oil, all the finished recipes in this book look (and largely taste) like regular cute-looking cupcakes! So do keep them well out of the reach of minors, or anyone who won't take kindly to an unexpected dose of the magic herb.

STORAGE ADVICE

You can store the infused oil in its original bottle if you like, but keep it in a cupboard out of the light, which can lower its potency. When you want to use it, shake well first.

I

I In a large, heavy saucepan, heat the oil over medium heat until hot but not boiling (it must not boil at any time). Lower the heat to keep it at a steady temperature.

2 Grind the marijuana as for the Boosted Butter (see page 12). Gradually shake it into the pan, stirring as you go until any lumps are dissolved.

3 Maintain that steady temperature for 2 hours. Keep an eye on it for the first half hour or so, stirring every 10 minutes. If it starts to boil, remove the pan from the heat and let it cool down a bit, and turn the heat down slightly. Do this a couple of times until you find the right heat. After a while the oil may turn a little bit green or brown due to the resin extraction; that's fine.

4 After 2 hours, remove the pan from the heat, let cool for about a half hour, then strain the liquid through a sieve or cheesecloth a couple of times and store. Discard the solids.

4

DON'T CARBONIZE IT

Although heating cannabis through the cooking process is proven to release more cannabinoids, overcooking (or exposing to extreme heat) will destroy much of the THC. Yikes! So pay close attention to the cooking temperatures in the recipes. They have been tested for optimum effectiveness.

Get Dosed!

The biggest mistake you can make with ganja gastronomy is the dosage. No one's expecting you to meet French patisserie standards, and if your finished cupcakes are a little messy, nobody will care as long as everyone gets pleasantly wasted. But woe betide you, should you mess up the special ingredient.

Measurements are based on the dosage for an experienced adult stoner of average weight, about 160 pounds (72 kilos). Because these weights are approximate, please experiment with dosage levels for people of different weights and experience. All recipes are calculated on the basis of a "normal" dosage (see sample calculation, page 19).

Too little, and you wait in vain for a high that never arrives; too much, and you could be tripping over your party guests on the floor for days afterward.

A single dose (that's per person, or per serving) is roughly half a teaspoon of ground weed or hash. But as we've noted, you're not using ground ganja directly in these recipes. So study the equivalent charts shown here and serve the cupcake treats accordingly. Friends with a sweet tooth and the raving munchies may not be willing to stop at just one cupcake, or even just two! You may need to hold some cupcakes in reserve (maybe under lock and key?). And please note that these figures are only a *basic* guide. The degree to which any individual is affected is the result of numerous variables: the ingredients used; the way the recipe has been prepared; the quality of the dope; and the person's weight, metabolism, state of mind, and experience of cannabis use.

★ If you just wanna cut to the chase and get those cupcakes made, you can use untreated ground cannabis instead of Boosted Butter or Souped-Up Sunflower Oil; keep in mind that the cupcake taste and texture will be affected. Add the powdered cannabis along with the dry ingredients (flour, sugar, and such) in each recipe.

TOKE TEST

If you're unsure or concerned about the potency of a particular strain of weed, don't just cook up your butter or oil, use the amount the recipe calls for, and hope for the best. Smoke a small sample first. If you get a huge buzz off a few tokes, then you know the effect will be similarly huge when baked, and you can distribute accordingly.

	MILD	NORMAL	EXTREME
Boosted Butter	1/2 tsp. (2.5 g)	1 tsp. (5 g)	1 1/2 tsp. (7.5 g)
Souped-Up Oil	1/2 tsp. (2.5 g)	1 tsp. (5 g)	1 1/2 tsp. (7.5 g)
★ Pot Powder	1/4 tsp. (.62 g)	1/2 tsp. (1.25 g)	3/4 tsp. (1.875 g)

What You'll Need

If you're reading this book, then you obviously want to get into cooking these sweet little beauties, but if you're not already an experienced home baker, you will need to equip yourself with some specific utensils. A simple and inexpensive way of doing this, particularly for the decorating stuff, is a starter set.

Muffin or cupcake pans or silicone molds—Most muffin pans tend to be sold as "muffin/cupcake" pans. (Standard muffin pans are deeper, with straighter sides, while true cupcake pans have shallower cups with more sloping sides.) All the recipes in this book will work in these and any other regular-sized pans, as long as you use the appropriate liners. Silicone molds make it easy to release the baked cakes. Because they're flexible, you'll need to set them on a cookie sheet for filling and baking. If you're buying metal muffin/cupcake pans for the first time and can afford it, go for a heavy-quality gauge—the heat spreads more evenly than in thin, flimsy pans.

Paper baking cups/liners—These come in a variety of colors and patterns; they help make the finished cupcakes look more attractive, and you don't have to grease the pans.

Measuring cups, measuring **spoons**, and **weighing scales**—Exact measurements are essential! Think of baking as chemistry, with ingredients interacting to make the cupcakes rise, brown, and, magically, turn from liquid batter to solid (yet moist), crumbly cake.

Mixing bowl—Use bowls that are roomy enough to mix all the ingredients without the batter slopping over the edge or spattering when you stir or beat. You'll need small, medium, and large bowls for mixing parts of the cake batter, making frosting, and so on. For melting chocolate you'll need a heatproof bowl to set over hot water on a burner.

Wooden spoon—For beating the batter.

Whisk—A balloon whisk or hand-held rotary whisk speeds up whisking ingredients such as egg whites and cream.

Hand-held electric whisk or food mixer—Not essential, but useful, as it relieves you of the hard work of hand beating or whisking.

Strainer or sifter—For evenly sifting together the flour and other dry ingredients. Use a small strainer for sifting the confectioners' sugar.

Rubber spatula—For scraping every last bit of batter from the mixing bowl, and also useful for folding in dry ingredients.

Wire cooling rack—To allow the steam to escape from the hot cupcakes and keep them from becoming soggy. You can also use the rack of a broiler pan.

Sharp knife—For cutting out shapes from decorator icing and cutting off cupcake tops.

Grater—For grating carrots, chocolate, nutmeg, and the like.

Piping nozzles—For piping butter-cream or frosting on the cakes. You'll need a small round tip to create small dots, straight lines, and outlines; a larger round tip for writing; and a star tip for stars, swirls, and decorative borders.

Cookie cutters—For cutting rounds from decorator icing for the top of cakes (dip in confectioners' sugar to prevent them sticking to the icing).

Pastry bag—Can be made of fabric or plastic; you can also buy disposable bags. Or use a plastic bag with a corner cut off.

Pastry brush—For brushing on hot jam or a thin coating of frosting.

Small rolling pin—Not essential, but makes rolling out small amounts of decorator icing easier to do.

Small palette knife—For spreading frosting and buttercream.

Small artist's brush—For painting on decorations.

A NOTE ON THE RECIPES

The recipes that follow use a quantity of prepared Boosted Butter (sometimes supplemented with plain butter) or Souped-Up Sunflower Oil. Dosage levels are measured in teaspoons per person (refer to the dosage table on page 17). To work out the quantity of chronic provided, you need to know the number of teaspoons in a cup (or portion thereof) of Boosted Butter—that is, 1 cup = 48 tsp.; 1/2 cup = 24 tsp.; 1/4 cup = 12 tsp., and so on. Also, the number of teaspoons in 1 tablespoon of Souped-Up Sunflower Oil (3). Divide the teaspoon total by the number of cakes—e.g., 12 teaspoons divided by 12 cupcakes = 1 tsp. per cake. Sound doable?

chapter **2**

CHOCO LOCO

This chapter is chocoholic nirvana. We've got light chocolate, we've got dark chocolate; we've got white chocolate, and we've got spicy—plus fudge and caramel toppings, too. But before you get all Willy Wonka, it's also a chapter that bears close scrutiny, cuz the first two recipes contain all the core info you need for future baking. So have fun, cheferinos, but don't go too loco with all that canna-cocoa!

Black Forest Cupcakes

Black Hole of Your Mind

Makes
12
cupcakes

Using the principal ingredients of the patisserie classic Black Forest Gateau, chocolate and cherries, these are literally the cakes "with the cherry on top." Bonus: the wooded mountain range in southwestern Germany that gives the dessert its name offers secluded spots, great for a weekend smoking session in the RV.

Difficulty:
Easy

Makin' Time:
25 minutes

Bakin' Time:
20 minutes

¼ cup (60 g) butter plus ¼ cup (60 g) Boosted Butter (page 12), at room temperature

½ cup (110 g) superfine sugar

¾ cup (85 g) self-rising flour

¼ cup (25 g) cocoa powder

Pinch of baking powder

2 eggs

3–4 tablespoons kirsch

CHOCOLATE TOPPING:

¾ cup (120 g) chocolate chips

¾ cup (150 g) unsalted butter, at room temperature

1 ⅓ cups (160 g) confectioners' sugar

1 teaspoon vanilla extract

DECORATION:

12 cherries, with stems

Confectioners' sugar

1 Once you've relocated the kitchen after last night's session, preheat the oven to 375°F (190°C/gas mark 5). Line a 12-cup muffin pan with paper baking cups.

2 In a large mixing bowl, whisk together the Boosted Butter, sugar, flour, cocoa, baking powder, and eggs until smooth and blended.

3 Spoon the mixture into the baking cups.

4 Bake (while you retire to the smoking den) until the cupcakes are well risen and firm to the touch, 15–20 minutes.

SLOW MELT . . .
When you're melting chocolate and/or butter in a bowl, be careful not to let the bottom of the bowl touch the simmering liquid, or the melting ingredients could separate.

5 Let cool in the pan for 5 minutes, then remove from the pan and place on a wire rack to cool completely.

7 To make the topping, melt the chocolate chips in a heatproof bowl over a pan of simmering (not boiling) water. Remove from the heat and let cool to room temperature.

6 Pierce the cupcakes with a skewer or fork and carefully pour about a teaspoon of kirsch over each. Keep your focus: you're at the halfway point.

8 In a mixing bowl, beat the butter with an electric mixer or by hand until smooth and creamy.

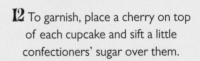

9 Sift in the confectioners' sugar and beat until light and fluffy. Then beat in the vanilla.

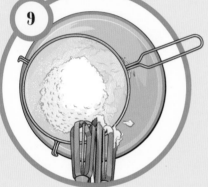

11 Spoon the mixture into a pastry bag and pipe a swirl onto the top of each cupcake. (And you might take this opportunity to tip your head back and squirt some of the mixture into your mouth.) If you don't have a pastry bag, simply spread the frosting with a table knife or spatula.

10 Add the chocolate and whisk until well blended. Continue whisking until smooth.

12 To garnish, place a cherry on top of each cupcake and sift a little confectioners' sugar over them.

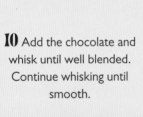

25

Rich Chocolate Cupcakes

Get Rich or Die Tryin'

Makes 12 cupcakes

Fiddy Cent's favorite (possibly), and heaven for the chocolate lover—chocolate cupcakes topped with chocolate frosting. So, after you've eaten the lot, lie back with a big reefer and count your bills. (Electricity, credit card, rather than Benjamins in your case, unfortunately.)

Difficulty:
Easy

Makin' Time:
25 minutes

Bakin' Time:
25 minutes

1 cup (150 g) all-purpose flour

1 tablespoon baking powder

Pinch of salt (ouch!)

3/4 cup (150 g) sugar

4 ounces (110 g) unsweetened chocolate

2/3 cup (150 g) butter plus 1/4 cup (60 g) Boosted Butter (page 12)

4 eggs, beaten

1 teaspoon vanilla extract

CHOCOLATE FROSTING:

2 ounces (50 g) unsweetened chocolate

1/2 cup (115 g) butter

1 heaped cup (150 g) confectioners' sugar

1 teaspoon vanilla extract

Milk

WHITE FROSTING:

1/2 cup (60 g) confectioners' sugar

Water

CANNABIS LEAVES:

4 ounces (115 g) green decorator icing

Cornstarch or confectioners' sugar, for dusting

MINI HASH BARS:

8 ounces (225 g) brown decorator icing

2 Sift the flour, baking powder, and salt into a large mixing bowl. Stir in the sugar. OK, now you're cooking—literally.

1 Preheat the oven to 400°F (200°C/gas mark 6). Line a 12-muffin pan with paper baking cups.

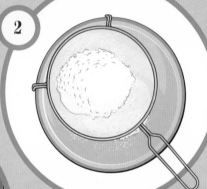

3 Melt the chocolate and Boosted Butter in a heatproof bowl set over a pan of simmering (not boiling) water.

4 Remove from the heat and stir into the flour mixture.

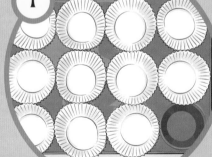

5 Add the eggs and vanilla extract to the mixture and stir until only just combined. The mixture will be lumpy, but don't worry (be happy)!

6 Spoon it into the prepared pan.

7 Bake until well risen and firm, 20–25 minutes. Time for you to fit in an episode of *South Park*.

OVERMIX? NIX

When the recipe instructions indicate that the batter should still be lumpy when you put it into the pan, take care not to overmix it, which can make the finished cupcakes dense and tough.

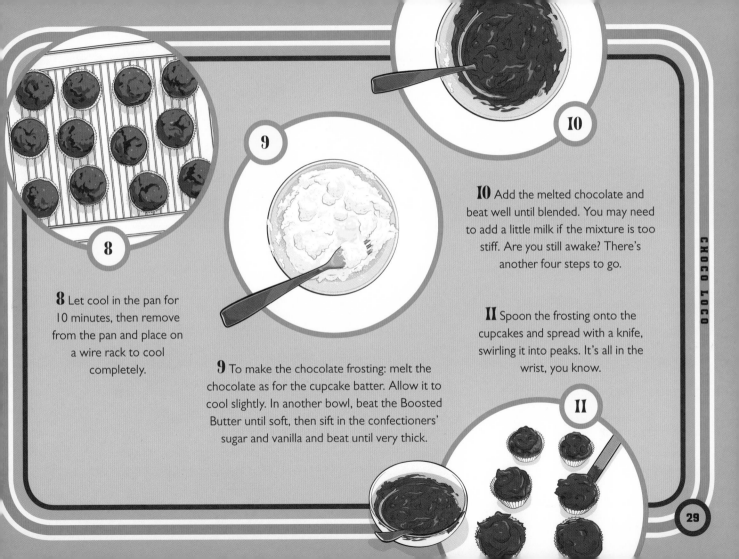

8 Let cool in the pan for 10 minutes, then remove from the pan and place on a wire rack to cool completely.

9 To make the chocolate frosting: melt the chocolate as for the cupcake batter. Allow it to cool slightly. In another bowl, beat the Boosted Butter until soft, then sift in the confectioners' sugar and vanilla and beat until very thick.

10 Add the melted chocolate and beat well until blended. You may need to add a little milk if the mixture is too stiff. Are you still awake? There's another four steps to go.

11 Spoon the frosting onto the cupcakes and spread with a knife, swirling it into peaks. It's all in the wrist, you know.

12 To make the white frosting, sift the confectioners' sugar into a bowl and gradually stir in a little water until smooth and thick. Dribble the frosting randomly over the cupcakes. (Then dribble down your chin at the prospect of diving into these beauties.)

14 To make the hash bars, cut the brown decorator icing into small bars. There's no need to roll out the decorator icing, as the block will be the required thickness. Place a mini hash bar on top of the chocolate frosting and attach a leaf to each bar using a little water. Leave to set. Don't get the hash bars mixed up with your kosher stash.

13 To make the cannabis leaf motif, cut out a stencil of the leaf to fit the top of the cake as shown. On a surface dusted with cornstarch or confectioners' sugar, roll the green decorator icing out thinly. Cut out the leaf shapes with a sharp knife (mind those pinkies).

Chocolate Fudge Cupcakes

Death by Chocolate

These chocolate cupcakes are topped with a wonderful mouthwatering chocolate fudge frosting. "Death by chocolate" reminds us of Mae West's classic observation: "Too much of a good thing is wonderful." Mae would approve of these.

Difficulty:
Easy

Makin' Time:
30 minutes

Bakin' Time:
25 minutes

Makes
12
cupcakes

1 cup (150 g) all-purpose flour

1 tablespoon baking powder

Pinch of salt

¾ cup (150 g) light brown sugar

4 ounces (110 g) semi-sweet chocolate

⅔ cup (150 g) butter plus ¼ cup (60 g) Boosted Butter (page 12)

4 eggs, beaten

1 teaspoon vanilla extract

CHOCOLATE FUDGE FROSTING:

¾ cup (120 g) chopped semi-sweet chocolate

⅔ cup (150 g) butter

1 ⅓ cups (160 g) confectioners' sugar

1 teaspoon vanilla extract

Milk

CANNABIS LEAVES:

4 ounces (115 g) green decorator icing

Cornstarch or confectioners' sugar, for dusting

Follow the instructions on page 30, opposite, to make 12 leaves

1 Preheat the oven to 400°F (200°C/gas mark 6). Line a 12-cup muffin pan with paper baking cups. Sift the flour, baking powder, and salt into a mixing bowl. Stir in the sugar.

3 Remove from the heat and let cool slightly. Stir into the flour mixture. Add the eggs and vanilla extract to the mixture and stir until only just combined. It will be lumpy!

2

2 Melt the chocolate and Boosted Butter in a heatproof bowl set over a pan of simmering (not boiling) water.

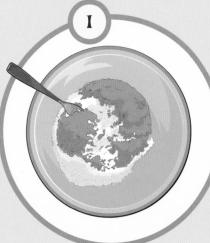

1

3

5

4

5 To make the frosting: melt the chocolate in a clean heatproof bowl set over a pan of simmering (not boiling) water. Remove from the heat and let cool slightly. Beat the butter in a bowl until soft. Then gradually sift in the confectioners' sugar. Beat well until smooth. Add the vanilla and stir in the melted chocolate until smooth. If the mixture is too stiff, add a little more milk.

6 Spread the frosting on top of the cupcakes. Top with the cannabis leaves.

6

4 Spoon into the prepared pan. Bake until risen and springy to the touch, 20–25 minutes—time enough to watch a bit of Cartoon Network. Let cool in the pan for 5 minutes, then remove from the pan and place on a wire rack to cool completely.

SIFT IT SLOW 'N' GOOD
When using confectioners' sugar, it is always best to sift it first to eliminate the lumps, which tend to persist even when mixed with liquid.

Chocolate Chili Cupcakes

Mexican Mayhem

As the Aztecs knew, the taste of chocolate is actually enhanced by the kick of chili. It might seem like a strange flavor combo, but, as Paula Abdul used to tell us, opposites attract, and if chefs are still using it after all this time, it must be so. You can find chili-spiced chocolate at a good natural foods or specialty foods market.

Difficulty:
Easy

Makin' Time:
15 minutes

Bakin' Time:
20 minutes

1 ¾ cups (250 g) all-purpose flour

¼ cup (25 g) cocoa powder

1 tablespoon baking powder

½ teaspoon chili powder

½ cup (100 g) sugar

2 eggs

3 ½ tablespoons sunflower oil plus 3 ½ tablespoons Souped-Up Sunflower Oil (page 15)

1 cup (225 ml) milk

¾ cup (75 g) grated chili-flavored chocolate

BUTTERSCOTCH CREAM:

½ cup (100 g) sugar

2 tablespoons water

Pinch of salt

1 ⅔ cups (400 ml) heavy cream

LEAVE WELL ENOUGH ALONE

When cooking sugar as for the butterscotch cream, after you have stirred once to dissolve the sugar, it is important not to stir it again, as this may cause the sugar to recrystallize, giving a grainy result.

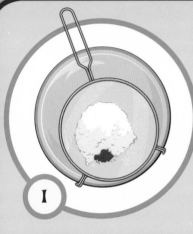

1

1 Preheat the oven to 400°F (200°C/gas mark 6). Line a 12-cup muffin pan with paper baking cups. Sift the flour, cocoa, baking powder, and chili powder into a mixing bowl. Stir in the sugar.

2 Whisk together the eggs and oil in a separate bowl until frothy, then whisk in the milk.

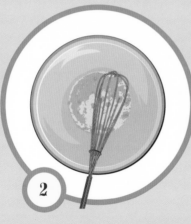

2

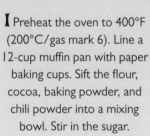

3

3 Stir into the dry ingredients until just blended. The batter will be slightly lumpy. Gently stir in the grated chocolate.

4 Spoon the batter into the prepared pan. Bake until risen and springy to the touch, 20–22 minutes. Let cool in the pan for 5 minutes, then remove from the pan and place on a wire rack to cool completely.

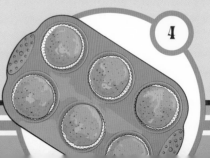

4

5 To make the butterscotch cream, heat the sugar, water, and salt in a pan over medium heat, stirring once, until the sugar is dissolved. Continue cooking, but do not stir, until the sugar caramelizes and turns golden amber, 8–10 minutes. Remove from the heat.

6 Slowly pour the cream into the pan of caramelized sugar, carefully, as it will spatter. Heat gently, stirring until combined. Pour the butterscotch cream into a mixing bowl and allow to cool. It'll be seriously tempting just to eat this mix as it is, but resist. Chill the cream in the refrigerator for about 40 minutes (while you chill in another room) until cold, stirring occasionally.

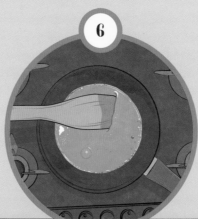

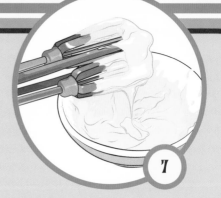

7 Whisk the chilled butterscotch cream until soft peaks form.

8 Spoon this into a pastry bag and pipe onto the tops of the cupcakes.

Spiced Chocolate Cupcakes with Caramel Sauce and Ice Cream

Calorie Overload

A touch of mixed spice gives these chocolate cupcakes an exotic flavor, complemented by a dreamy caramel sauce and ice cream. So settle back on your couch and take a perfect trip to munchie heaven.

Difficulty:
Medium

Makin' Time:
30 minutes

Bakin' Time:
25 minutes

2/3 cup (80 g) grated semi-sweet chocolate (Tip: it's easier to grate chocolate if you chill it first.)

1 3/4 cups (200 g) all-purpose flour

2 tablespoons cocoa powder

1 tablespoon pumpkin spice

1 tablespoon baking powder

2 eggs

1/4 cup (50 g) sugar

1/5 cup (50 ml) Souped-Up Sunflower Oil (page 15)

1/5 cup (50 ml) milk, plus more if needed

CARAMEL SAUCE:

1 cup (225 g) superfine sugar

1 1/2 tablespoons water

1/3 cup (80 g) diced butter

1/2 cup (120 ml) heavy cream

Pinch of salt

TO SERVE:

Ice cream

Makes 12 cupcakes

1

1 Preheat the oven to 400°F (200°C/gas mark 6). Line a 12-cup muffin pan with paper baking cups. Mix the chocolate with the sifted flour, cocoa powder, mixed spice, and baking powder in a bowl.

2 In a large bowl, beat the eggs with the sugar and oil. Quickly beat the flour mixture into the eggs, adding as much milk as required to get a dropping consistency: a small amount of the mixture will fall from the spoon if gently shaken (but if you shake it vigorously, it'll go everywhere, ya dummy).

2

3

3 Spoon the batter into the prepared pan. Bake until risen and baked through, 20–25 minutes. Test with a wooden toothpick: if it comes out clean, the cupcakes are done. (Hang onto that toothpick; it's useful for rescuing badly rolled joints.) Let cool in the pan for 5 minutes, then remove from the pan and place on a wire rack to cool completely.

4 To make the caramel sauce, heat the sugar and water in a saucepan over low heat until the sugar has dissolved. Increase the heat and cook until the mixture starts to brown.

5 Remove from the heat. Stir in the butter and cream until the butter has melted. Add the salt and cook over very low heat, stirring, until smooth.

6 To serve, put the cupcakes on serving plates and spoon the sauce over them. Place a scoop of ice cream alongside each cupcake.

STAY OFF THE HOOCH

Be very careful when cooking sugar solutions, as they get very hot—much hotter even than boiling water—and can give you a very bad burn. So make sure you're reasonably sober.

Chocolate, Pecan, and Marshmallow Cupcakes

Triple Whammy

We all remember roasting marshmallows over the campfire while camping (except for those of us who went to Fat Camp). These cupcakes, with their combination of marshmallows, chocolate, and pecans, are like s'mores but all grown up.

Difficulty:
Easy

Makin' Time:
25 minutes

Bakin' Time:
25 minutes

Makes 12 cupcakes

³/₈ cup (90 g) butter plus ¹/₄ cup (60 g) Boosted Butter (page 12), at room temperature

1 ¹/₂ cups (300 g) superfine sugar

3 eggs, beaten

1 cup (250 ml) milk

2 cups (275 g) all-purpose flour

Pinch of salt

1 teaspoon baking soda

¹/₂ cup (55 g) cocoa powder

CHOCOLATE FROSTING:

³/₄ cup (110 g) chopped semi-sweet chocolate

²/₃ cup (150 g) butter, at room temperature

1 ¹/₂ cups (160 g) confectioners' sugar

1 teaspoon vanilla extract

DECORATION:

³/₄ cup (110 g) chopped semi-sweet chocolate

³/₄ cup (110 g) chopped pecans

Mini marshmallows

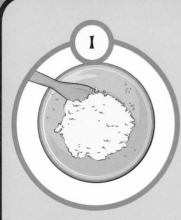

4 Spoon into the prepared pan.

3 Sift in the flour, salt, baking soda, and cocoa. Stir well to mix.

5 Bake until a skewer or wooden cocktail stick inserted into the center comes out clean, 20–25 minutes. Allow to cool in the pan for 5 minutes, then remove from the pan and place on a wire rack to cool completely. Man, that's cool. Roll and smoke a single skin while you assess your progress.

1 Preheat the oven to 350°F (180°C/gas mark 4). Line a 12-cup muffin pan with paper baking cups. Beat the Boosted Butter and sugar in a mixing bowl until soft and creamy.

2 Beat in the eggs and milk (to within an inch of their lives!).

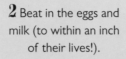

6

7 In a large mixing bowl, beat the Boosted Butter with an electric mixer or by hand until smooth and creamy. Beat in the vanilla and melted chocolate, and then beat on low speed until well blended. Increase the speed and beat until the mixture is smooth and glossy. Don't get any on the ceiling.

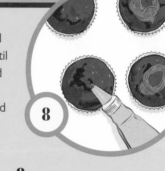

8

6 To make the frosting, melt the chocolate in a heatproof bowl set over a pan of simmering (not boiling) water. Remove from the heat and let cool to room temperature.

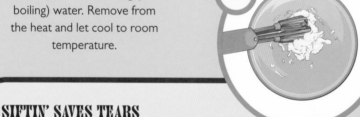

7

8 Put the mixture in a pastry bag with a small tip and pipe (or simply spoon) the frosting onto the cupcakes.

9 Decorate with the chopped chocolate, pecans, and mini marshmallows.

SIFTIN' SAVES TEARS

When making a frosting or other mixture containing confectioners' sugar that will be piped onto a cupcake, be sure to sift it into the mix, as any clumps—even quite small ones—can block the piping nozzle. (Although you can always try to suck them out.)

9

White Chocolate Cupcakes with Smiley Faces

Makes
12
cupcakes

Grinnin' from Ear to Ear

The refined deliciousness of white chocolate combined with the tang of buttermilk gives these cupcakes a subtly intriguing flavor, assuming you're not too stoned to notice. When the smiley faces start talking to ya, you know you've had too many. Add food coloring to the white frosting to create different colored faces. Trippy.

Difficulty:
Easy

Makin' Time:
15 minutes

Bakin' Time:
20 minutes

¹/₄ cup (60 g) butter plus ¹/₄ cup (60 g) Boosted Butter

³/₄ cup (175 g) superfine sugar

2 eggs, beaten

1 teaspoon vanilla extract

2 ¹/₄ cups (325 g) self-rising flour

¹/₂ cup (125 ml) buttermilk

1 ²/₃ cups (275 g) finely chopped white chocolate

WHITE CHOCOLATE FROSTING:

6 ounces (175 g) white chocolate

¹/₄ cup (60 ml) light cream

Food coloring (optional)

DECORATION:

Chocolate jelly beans

Thin red licorice strips, cut into 12 pieces

1 Preheat the oven to 325°F (160°C/gas mark 3). Line a 12-cup muffin pan with paper baking cups. Beat the Boosted Butter and sugar in a mixing bowl until soft and creamy. Gradually beat in the eggs and vanilla until blended.

2 Alternating portions, fold in a third of the flour and then a third of the buttermilk, stirring after each addition until just combined. Gently stir in the chocolate.

3 Spoon the batter into the muffin cups. Bake until golden and well risen, 20–23 minutes. (Anyone for a quick bowl in the meantime?) Allow to cool in the pan for 5 minutes, then remove from the pan and place on a wire rack to cool completely.

4 To make the frosting, heat the chocolate and cream in a heatproof bowl over a pan of simmering (not boiling) water until the chocolate has melted.

5 If you want to make different colored faces, divide the frosting into smaller bowls and stir the food coloring of your choice into each. Be sure to reserve some white frosting. Let cool slightly until thickened.

6 Spread the white chocolate frosting over the cupcakes. Press the chocolate jelly beans into the frosting for the eyes and noses. Press on the red licorice strips to form a smiley mouth on each cupcake. Let the frosting set until ready to serve.

MELTDOWN ALERT!

When melting chocolate over a pan of hot water, try to ensure that no water gets into the chocolate, as this can cause it to "seize"—that is, turn grainy and/or clumpy.

CHOCO LOCO

chapter **3**

DAINTY
DOPESTER
CUPCAKES

It's time to get in touch with your feminine side, cuz the cupcakes in this chapter are so delicate and dainty that you might as well make them while wearing a poofy skirt and listening to One Direction. This section is essential to your cupcake training, so you female readers are in luck. Dudes, rest assured that your final results will impress the ladies. And you can smoke some chronic while you wait for your cupcakes to rise.

Vanilla Ice Cupcakes

Ice, Ice, Baby

Make like Robert Van Winkle and take it "to the extreme" with these perfect little vanilla-flavored cupcakes with vanilla buttercream topping and emphatic icing roll-ups. And with some early '90s hip hop on the sound system, you can check out the hook while his DJ revolves it . . . as you're lining your pan with paper baking cups. #streetcred

Difficulty:
Easy

Makin' Time:
15 minutes

Bakin' Time:
20 minutes

1 1/2 cups (225 g) self-rising flour

Pinch of salt

1/4 cup (60 g) butter plus 1/4 cup (60 g) Boosted Butter (page 12), softened

1/2 cup (110 g) superfine sugar

2 eggs

1 teaspoon vanilla extract

VANILLA BUTTERCREAM:

3/4 cup (175 g) butter

3 cups (350 g) confectioners' sugar

1–2 tablespoon(s) milk

1/2 teaspoon vanilla extract

DOOBIES:

4 ounces (110 g) brown or green decorator icing

6 ounces (175 g) white decorator icing

1 Preheat the oven to 375°F (190°C/gas 5). Line a 12-cup muffin pan with paper baking cups. Put all the cupcake ingredients in a mixing bowl and beat until very smooth.

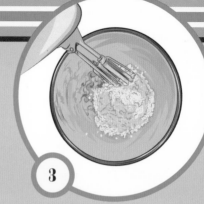

2 Spoon the batter into the prepared pan; it will be quite thick and hard to level in the cups, but don't worry; it will level up when heated in the oven. Bake until well risen, just firm to the touch, and lightly golden, 15–20 minutes. Allow to cool in the pan for 5 minutes, then remove from the pan and place on a wire rack to cool completely.

3 To make the buttercream, beat the butter with an electric mixer or by hand until fluffy, 2–3 minutes. Sift in the confectioners' sugar and beat well. Mix in the milk and vanilla extract, and whisk until the cream is light and fluffy. With all this beating and whisking, I think you've earned a joint break.

KEEP THAT NOZZLE CLEAR

Remember to sift in the confectioners' sugar for the buttercream, as clumps can block the pastry bag nozzle.

4 Spoon the buttercream into a pastry bag fitted with a small tip and pipe swirls onto the tops of the cupcakes.

5 To make the doobies: roll out both the decorator icings separately on nonstick baking paper. Cut the brown decorator icing into 12 pieces and roll between the palms of your hands to form little logs. Place each log on a small amount—er, a rolling paper size—of white icing and roll it up to resemble a doobie.

6 Set one doobie on top of each cupcake. (Don't try to light 'em.)

Carrot Cupcakes with Cream Cheese Frosting

What's Up, Doc?

These are so quaint they would be ideal for your grandma's next coffee gathering—if only they weren't laced with Boosted Butter. As with ordinary carrot cake, the grated carrot mostly dissolves into the batter during baking, with a wonderfully moist result. And if you eat at least three in one sitting, you will be able to see in the dark—or at least think you can.

Difficulty:
Easy

Makin' Time:
30 minutes

Bakin' Time:
20 minutes

1 ½ cups (300 g) packed light brown sugar

1 ¾ cups (250 g) self-rising flour

1 teaspoon baking soda

1 teaspoon ground cinnamon

2 eggs

⅔ cup (150 ml) sunflower oil

4 cups (200 g) grated carrots

CREAM CHEESE FROSTING:

¼ cup (60 g) butter plus ¼ cup (60 g) Boosted Butter (page 12)

1 ½ cups (300 g) cream cheese

1 cup (115 g) confectioners' sugar

1 teaspoon vanilla extract

1 Preheat the oven to 350°F (180°C/gas mark 4). Line a 12-cup muffin pan with paper baking cups. Mix together the sugar, flour, baking soda, and cinnamon in a mixing bowl.

2 In another bowl, whisk together the eggs and oil. Add to the dry ingredients along with the grated carrots and stir until just blended.

KEEP IT FRESH

Ground cinnamon loses its flavor quite quickly, so make sure yours is fairly fresh—or get a new jar; it's a lot cheaper than some of the other ingredients!

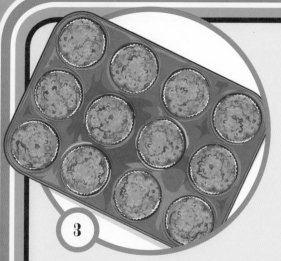

3

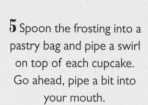

4 To make the frosting, beat the Boosted Butter until soft, then beat in the cream cheese until blended. Sift in the confectioners' sugar, then stir in the vanilla until smooth.

5

3 Spoon the batter into the prepared pan and bake until risen and golden, 20–23 minutes. Let cool in the pan for 5 minutes, then remove from the pan and place on a wire rack to cool some more, until they're cooler than LL Cool J.

4

5 Spoon the frosting into a pastry bag and pipe a swirl on top of each cupcake. Go ahead, pipe a bit into your mouth.

Espresso Cupcakes

Give Me a Hit

These little beauties make the perfect combination for a breakfast snack—a caffeine OD coupled with a trippy sativa will have you buzzing until the following morning.

Difficulty:
Easy

Makin' Time:
30 minutes

Bakin' Time:
20 minutes

Makes 12 cupcakes

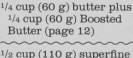

¹/4 cup (60 g) butter plus ¹/4 cup (60 g) Boosted Butter (page 12)

¹/2 cup (110 g) superfine (and dandy) sugar

1 cup (150 g) self-rising flour

Pinch of salt

2 eggs

3 tablespoons (45 ml) cold espresso coffee

COFFEE-BOOSTED BUTTERCREAM:

¹/2 cup (110 g) butter

2 ¹/4 cups (250 g) confectioners' sugar

1–2 tablespoons instant espresso coffee powder dissolved in 1 tablespoon hot water

I Preheat the oven to 350°F (180°C/gas mark 4). Line a 12-cup muffin pan with paper baking cups. In a mixing bowl, beat the Boosted Butter, sugar, flour, salt, eggs, and coffee until smooth.

EXTRA SHOTS?
You can adjust the strength of the coffee for the cupcake batter according to your taste.

2 Spoon the batter into the prepared pan and bake until well risen, golden, and beginning to feel firm when lightly touched on the top, 16–20 minutes. Allow to cool in the pan for 5 minutes, then remove from the pan and place on a wire rack to cool completely. Time for a cup of coffee and a reefer?

4 Spoon the buttercream into a pastry bag and pipe a swirl onto each cupcake. Chill (that's the cupcakes and you) until ready to serve.

3 To make the buttercream, beat the Boosted Butter in a bowl until soft. Sift in the confectioners' sugar and beat until light and fluffy. Beat in the coffee until smooth.

Tiramisu Cupcakes

Bellisimo

Based on everyone's favorite Italian dessert, these have a mascarpone topping so delicious you'll want to make double the quantity and eat the extra with spoons. Tiramisu translates as "pick me up" or "make me happy," which sounds like some of the drugs you like to imbibe. So how come this is legal and your stash is not? Must write to your representatives about that . . .

MASCARPONE CREAM TOPPING:

3/4 cup (175 g) butter

2 3/4 cups (300 g) confectioners' sugar

1 cup (225 g) mascarpone

TO FINISH:

4 tablespoons unsweetened cocoa powder

Difficulty:
Easy

Makin' Time:
30 minutes

Bakin' Time:
20 minutes

Makes 12 cupcakes

1/4 cup (60 g) butter plus 1/4 cup (60 g) Boosted Butter (page 12)

1/2 cup (110 g) packed light brown sugar

1 cup (150 g) self-rising flour

1 tablespoon cocoa powder

1 tablespoon instant espresso coffee powder

2 large eggs

1–2 tablespoons milk

THE X FACTOR
If you can't find mascarpone, ordinary cream cheese will do, but it won't have the *gustoso*! factor.

2 Spoon the batter into the baking cups and bake until golden and springy, 18–20 minutes. (Don't try bouncing them off the floor; we're not talking that kinda springy). Allow to cool in the pan for 5 minutes, then remove from the pan and place on a wire rack to cool completely.

3 To make the mascarpone cream, in a large mixing bowl beat the Boosted Butter until soft, then sift in the sugar. Gradually beat in the mascarpone until smooth and creamy.

4 Spoon a little mascarpone cream on top of each cupcake. Sift cocoa powder over the top just before serving.

1 Preheat the oven to 350°F (180°C/gas mark 4). Line a 12-cup muffin pan with paper baking cups. Beat all the cupcake ingredients in a mixing bowl until smooth. If the batter is too stiff, add a little more milk.

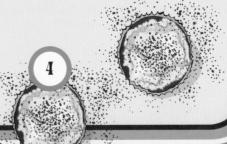

Smilin' Berry Cupcakes

Strawberry Fields Forever

You'll soon realize "nothing is real and [there's] nothing to get hung about" once you start eating these munchies. They're the perfect cupcakes for a picnic with your bong—or any outdoor session—on a summer's day.

Difficulty:
Easy

Makin' Time:
20 minutes

Bakin' Time:
25 minutes

Makes
12
cupcakes

¾ cup (170 g) butter plus ¼ cup (60 g) Boosted Butter (page 12), softened

1 cup (200 g) sugar

2 eggs

1 egg yolk

2 ½ cups (375 g) self-rising flour

½ teaspoon baking powder

⅓ cup (80ml) milk

TOPPING:

1 cup (240 ml) heavy cream

2 tablespoons superfine sugar (or to taste)

12 small- to medium-size hulled strawberries

I Preheat the oven to 350°F (180°C/ gas mark 4). Line a 12-cup muffin pan with paper baking cups. Put all the cupcake ingredients into a large mixing bowl and beat well until smooth.

2 Spoon the batter into the prepared pan and bake until risen and golden, 20–25 minutes. Allow to cool in the pan for 5 minutes, then remove from the pan and place on a wire rack to cool completely while you tend to other pressing business—like phoning your dealer.

A SCINTILLA OF VANILLA

If you like, you can add a little vanilla extract or vanilla seeds scraped from a vanilla bean pod to either the cupcake batter or the cream topping—or both!

4 Spoon some of the whipped cream on top of each of the cupcakes and nestle a strawberry into each mound of cream. Sweet.

3 To make the topping, beat the heavy cream with the sugar until it forms firm peaks.

chapter 4

FRUITY LOOPY

Real fruit is a food that some of you stoners out there may not encounter very often in your diet—er, jelly beans don't count. Most fruits are not only full of fiber and antioxidants, but they are also wonderfully sweet and tasty—an especially appropriate property for cupcakes—so let's embrace the fruitylicious world of cherries, apples, bananas, strawberries, and their many and varied kind.

Psychedelic Fresh Cherry Cupcakes

Granny Takes a Trip

Fresh cherries and marzipan make these a real taste treat, and the topping is a kaleidoscopic sensation. As British father of LSD, Humphry Osmond, wrote: "To fathom hell or soar angelic, just take a pinch of psychedelic." So dig in!

Difficulty:
Medium

Makin' Time:
20 minutes

Bakin' Time:
25 minutes

Makes
12
cupcakes

1/4 cup (60 g) butter plus 1/4 cup (60 g) Boosted Butter (page 12)

1/3 cup (80 g) superfine sugar

2 large eggs, beaten

1 cup (150 g) self-rising flour

1/2 teaspoon baking powder

1 tablespoon milk

4 ounces (110 g) marzipan, coarsely grated

1/2 cup (100 g) pitted, halved fresh cherries

I Preheat the oven to 350°F (180°C/gas mark 4). Line a 12-cup muffin pan with paper baking cups. In a mixing bowl, beat the Boosted Butter and sugar together until light and fluffy.

DECORATION:

12 ounces (350 g) white decorator icing

Confectioners' sugar, for dusting

3–4 tablespoons warmed apricot jelly

4–5 tubes different colored gel icing

2 Add the eggs, flour, baking powder, and milk, and beat well until thick and creamy. Gently fold the marzipan and cherries into the batter until blended.

3 Spoon the batter into the prepared pan and bake until risen and golden, 20–25 minutes. Allow to cool in the pan for 10 minutes, then remove from the pan and place on a wire rack to cool completely.

4 For the decoration, roll out the decorator icing on a surface lightly dusted with confectioners' sugar. Using a cookie cutter, cut out 12 rounds the same size as the cupcakes. Brush the decorator icing rounds with a little of the apricot jelly and place carefully on the cupcakes, pressing lightly. Now for the acid test . . .

DIY COOKIE CUTTER

If you haven't got a cookie cutter to make the icing rounds, you might be able to use the lid of a suitably sized jelly jar or something similar.

5 Using different-colored gel icing, pipe a series of concentric circles (that's like, circles within other circles) on each cupcake. Draw a wooden cocktail stick or toothpick through the gel to swirl the colors together. Now that's trippy.

Spiced Apricot Muffins

You're No Prune

These spicy fruit delights make a great post- or mid-session dessert, served with some whipped cream or ice cream. And they are so easy to make, even a simple stoner like you can crack it. But don't eat too many. The combination of spice and apricot (a known laxative) may mean that you spend more time sitting on the (other) pot.

Difficulty:
Easy

Makin' Time:
15 minutes

Bakin' Time:
30 minutes

1 heaped cup (150 g) all-purpose flour

2 teaspoons ground cinnamon

1/2 tablespoon baking powder

Pinch of salt

1/4 cup (55 g) superfine sugar

3/4 cup (110 g) chopped fresh apricots

1 large egg

1/2 cup (110 ml) milk

2 tablespoons (30 g) butter plus 2 tablespoons (30 g) Boosted Butter (page 12), melted

Makes
6
muffins

CUT JUST SO
Resist the temptation to cut the apricots too small or they'll probably turn to mush when the mixture is baked; you really want them to retain their juicy texture in the finished muffins.

1 Preheat the oven to 400°F (200°C/gas mark 6). Grease a 6-cup muffin pan (standard, not jumbo sized) with a little butter. Sift the flour, cinnamon, baking powder, and salt into a mixing bowl and stir in the sugar and apricots.

2 In another bowl, lightly whisk together the egg, milk, and Boosted Butter. Fold into the dry ingredients until just combined. The mixture will be lumpy.

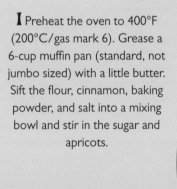

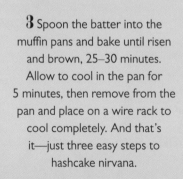

3 Spoon the batter into the muffin pans and bake until risen and brown, 25–30 minutes. Allow to cool in the pan for 5 minutes, then remove from the pan and place on a wire rack to cool completely. And that's it—just three easy steps to hashcake nirvana.

Cinnamon and Blueberry Muffins

Super Stoner Food

As quintessentially American as, er, blueberry pie, these muffins are just like the ones Mom used to make. Nutritionists rate blueberries as a superfood—one of those über-healthy foods like beets (but who eats those?) that ward off cancer and the like. Hey, any treat that satisfies the munchies, gets you high, *and* makes you healthier gets our vote!

Difficulty:
Easy

Makin' Time:
20 minutes

Bakin' Time:
20 minutes

Makes
12
muffins

2 cups (200 g) fresh or frozen, thawed blueberries

2 1/4 cups (325 g) all-purpose flour

1/4 cup (60 g) butter plus 1/4 cup (60 g) Boosted Butter (page 12)

3/4 cup (150 g) sugar

1 egg

2 teaspoons ground cinnamon

2 1/2 teaspoons baking powder

1/2 teaspoon baking soda

Pinch of salt

1 1/5 cups (300 ml) plain yogurt

I

I Preheat the oven to 350°F (180°C/gas mark 4). Line a 12-cup muffin pan with paper baking cups. Toss the blueberries in 2 tablespoons of the flour. Set aside.

2  Beat the Boosted Butter and sugar together in a mixing bowl until light and fluffy. Beat in the egg. Sift in the remaining flour and the cinnamon, baking powder, baking soda, and salt, and stir until just combined.

3 Gently stir the yogurt and blueberries into the mix. Spoon the batter into the prepared muffin pans. Now give your arm a rest, or you'll be too tired to roll any fatties later.

COATIN' THOSE BERRIES
Tossing the berries in flour before adding them to the muffin batter helps ensure that they don't all drift to the bottom of the muffins during baking.

4 Bake until well risen and firm, 20–25 minutes. Allow to cool in the pan for 10 minutes, then remove from the pan and place on a wire rack to cool completely.

Mini Cherry Cupcakes

Cheery Teensy Bites

While making these flavor sensations, it would be appropriate to think of Honest George Washington and that lame (sorry, heartwarming) story of the cherry tree. It might bring tears to your eyes . . . or is that the pain from dropping another hot rock in your lap?

Makes
24
mini
cupcakes

Difficulty:
Easy

Makin' Time:
15 minutes

Bakin' Time:
15 minutes

STAY FOCUSSED
Keep a careful eye on these if they're not done near the 15-minute mark, as they can overcook quickly.

¹/₃ cup (75 g) Boosted Butter (page 12)

¹/₃ cup (75 g) superfine sugar

2 eggs, beaten

³/₄ cup (100 g) self-rising flour

¹/₂ teaspoon almond extract

¹/₃ cup (75 g) chopped candied cherries

1 Preheat the oven to 350°F (180°C/gas mark 4). Line pans for 24 mini cupcakes with mini paper baking cups. Beat the Boosted Butter and sugar in a mixing bowl until light and fluffy. Gradually add the eggs, a little at a time, and Beat It . . . Michael Jackson style.

2 Sift in the flour and gently fold into the mixture. Stir in the almond extract and candied cherries.

3 Spoon the batter into the prepared pans and bake until golden and just firm to the touch, 12–15 minutes. Place on a wire rack to cool. Enjoy.

FRUITY LOOPY

Hummingbird Muffins

Soaring High

These flavor-packed muffins are based on the hummingbird cake traditional in the South since the mid-1800s—a dessert that usually has a cream cheese frosting. No one knows for sure how it got the name, but we can assure you that no actual hummingbirds are harmed in the making of this recipe.

Difficulty:
Easy

Makin' Time:
25 minutes

Bakin' Time:
30 minutes

Makes
12
muffins

3 1/4 cups (450 g) self-rising flour

1 teaspoon ground cinnamon

1 cup (225 g) superfine sugar

2 ripe bananas

2 eggs, beaten

1/4 cup (4 tablespoons) sunflower oil plus 1/4 cup (4 tablespoons) Souped-Up Sunflower Oil (page 15)

1 cup (150 g) chopped pecans

One 14 1/2-ounce (440 g) can crushed pineapple in natural juice, well drained

I

I Preheat the oven to 350°F (180°C/gas mark 4). Line a 12-cup muffin pan with paper baking cups. Sift the flour and cinnamon into a mixing bowl and stir in the sugar.

LEMON CREAM:

1 cup (225 g) unsalted butter

4 cups (450 g) confectioners' sugar

4–5 tablespoons lemon curd

Yellow food coloring

2 Peel the bananas and mash them until they're like you at the tail end of a Saturday night. Stir into the flour mixture together with the eggs, oil, pecans, and pineapple. Stir until the mixture is just combined, but still slightly lumpy.

3

4

3 Spoon the batter into the prepared pan and bake until risen and golden, 25–30 minutes. Allow to cool in the pan for 5 minutes, then remove from the pan and place on a wire rack to cool completely.

2

4 To make the lemon cream, beat the butter until creamy, then gradually sift in the confectioners' sugar and beat until smooth. Stir in the lemon curd and a few drops of yellow food coloring to give a nice pale yellow color.

5

5 Spread or pipe the lemon cream on top of the cupcakes. Then watch the gang hover around the table at serving time.

STRAIN 'N' DRAIN . . .
Make sure you drain the canned pineapple well, or the juices will make the cupcakes too soft.

Fruity Mini Brioche Cupcakes

Let Them Eat Cake

Ooh la la. Based on the classic French brioche, these fruity cupcakes are great for breakfast with a cup of hash tea or as a snack. Try splitting them across and spreading them with butter. "Ils sont délicieuses," as your French exchange student might say. Note that you need to start these a day ahead, as they need to rise overnight.

Difficulty:
Medium

Makin' Time:
20 minutes, plus 12 hours rising

Bakin' Time:
20 minutes

¹/₄ cup (60 g) very soft butter plus ³/₄ cup (165 g) very soft Boosted Butter (page 12)

2 tablespoons superfine sugar

4 eggs, divided

4 ¹/₂ cups (625 g) bread flour

¹/₂ teaspoon fast-acting yeast

1 teaspoon salt

⁷/₈ cup (200 ml) milk

¹/₂ cup (75 g) raisins

Makes
12
cupcakes

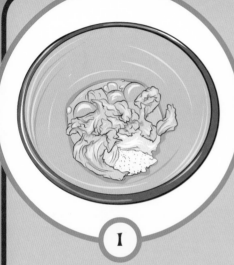

2 Add the flour, yeast, and salt, and mix briefly together. Pour in the milk and mix to a soft, sticky consistency. Stir in the raisins. There will be lumps of Boosted Butter in the mixture.

1

2

3

1 Beat together the Boosted Butter, sugar, and 3 of the eggs in a mixing bowl. The mixture will be lumpy.

3 Cover the bowl with a dishtowel and leave in a moderately warm place overnight. And so, with the rest of the evening your own, you might as well get wasted.

4 The next day—realistically, some time after lunch, once you've gotten your head together—preheat the oven to 375°F (190°C/gas mark 5). Grease a pan for 12 mini brioche or muffins. Drop small handfuls of the dough (which will be very sticky) into the pans—from a great height, if you like, to amuse yourself.

5 Beat the remaining egg and brush the tops of the brioches with it (this creates a nice glaze).

6 Bake until just browned on top, about 20 minutes. Allow to cool in the pan for 5 minutes, then remove from the pan and place on a wire rack to cool completely.

Rockin' Raspberry Muffins

Red Alert

Let's have a raspberry ripple of applause for these tasty muffins, which make an excellent dessert served with whipped cream or ice cream. Enjoy . . . then spend the next hour getting the seeds out of your teeth.

Difficulty:
Easy

Makin' Time:
15 minutes

Bakin' Time:
20 minutes

Makes 10 muffins

2 3/4 cups (400 g) all-purpose flour

1 tablespoon baking powder

1/2 cup (100 g) superfine sugar

1/4 cup (60 g) butter plus 1/4 cup (60 g) Boosted Butter (page 12), melted

2 large eggs

7/8 cup (200 ml) milk

1 cup (150 g) fresh or frozen, thawed raspberries

I Preheat the oven to 400°F (200°C/ gas mark 6). Line 10 cups of a 12-cup muffin pan with paper baking cups. Sift the flour and baking powder into a mixing bowl. Stir in the sugar.

2

3 Spoon the batter into the baking cups and bake until done, 15–20 minutes. Allow to cool in the pan for a few minutes, then remove from the pan and place on a wire rack to cool completely. Enjoy these with a lovely pot of "herbal" tea.

2 In another bowl, whisk together the butter, eggs, and milk. Pour into the dry ingredients and stir until just combined. Gently fold in the raspberries.

BERRY BREAKUP CRISIS?

Unless they are very unripe, the raspberries will break up completely as you stir them into the batter, which is fine.

Banana and Walnut Muffins

Fruit 'n' Nut

These muffins make the most of the natural sweetness of sticky bananas and the warm toastiness of the nuts. They're a bunch of fun to make, and they taste sublime. And when the Boosted Butter buzz has worn off, you can always trying smoking the banana peels. "They call me mellow yellow (quite rightly) . . ."

Difficulty:
Easy

Makin' Time:
20 minutes

Bakin' Time:
25 minutes

Makes
12
muffins

2 1/4 cups (325 g) self-rising flour

1 teaspoon baking powder

1/2 teaspoon baking soda

Pinch of salt

1 teaspoon ground cinnamon

1/2 cup (110 g) superfine sugar

2 eggs

1 teaspoon vanilla extract

1 tablespoon (15 g) butter plus 1/4 cup (60 g) Boosted Butter (page 12), melted

1/2 cup (125 ml) milk

2 very ripe bananas

1 cup (110 g) chopped walnuts

BANANA CREAM:

2 ripe bananas

1 cup (225 ml) heavy cream

4 tablespoons confectioners' sugar

4 tablespoons cream cheese, at room temperature

2 tablespoons freshly squeezed lemon juice

DECORATION:

Oreos, broken into pieces

M&Ms

1 Preheat the oven to 375°F (190°C/gas mark 5). Line a 12-cup muffin pan with paper baking cups. Sift the flour, baking powder, baking soda, salt, and cinnamon into a mixing bowl, then stir in the sugar.

2 Beat together the eggs, vanilla extract, Boosted Butter, and milk until combined. Mash the bananas well and stir into the egg mixture.

3 Make a well in the center of the dry ingredients and add the egg mixture along with the walnuts, stirring roughly with a fork (don't overmix) to form a thick, lumpy batter.

4 Spoon the batter into the prepared muffin cups and bake until the muffins are golden and risen and springy to the touch, 20–25 minutes. Allow to cool in the pan for 5 minutes, then remove from the pan and place on a wire rack to cool completely.

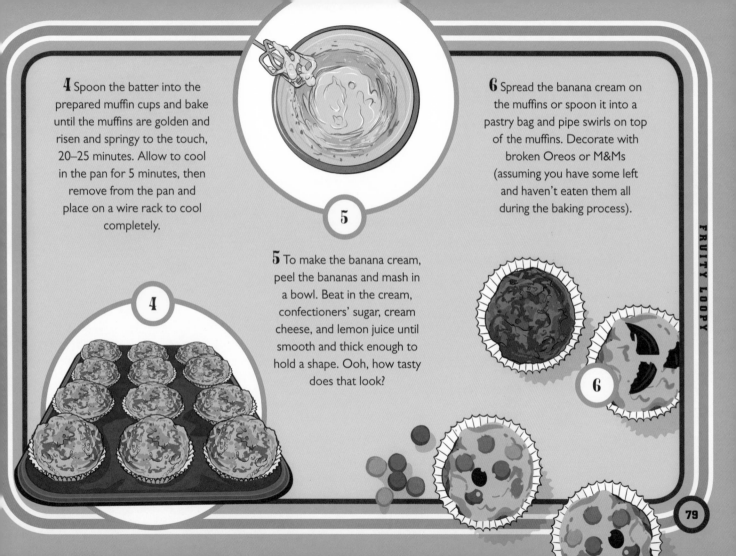

5

5 To make the banana cream, peel the bananas and mash in a bowl. Beat in the cream, confectioners' sugar, cream cheese, and lemon juice until smooth and thick enough to hold a shape. Ooh, how tasty does that look?

6 Spread the banana cream on the muffins or spoon it into a pastry bag and pipe swirls on top of the muffins. Decorate with broken Oreos or M&Ms (assuming you have some left and haven't eaten them all during the baking process).

4

6

Lemon and Poppy Seed Muffins

Zest Is Best

This delicious flavor combo owes its origins to the cakes served for breakfast on the Jewish holiday of Purim. But be warned: you'll be rightly cast as Judas if you try to sabotage your family's religious holiday with the pot-laced version of these cakes, and it's certainly inappropriate to smoke the poppy seeds.

Difficulty:
Easy

Makin' Time:
15 minutes

Bakin' Time:
22 minutes

Makes 12 muffins

2 cups (300 g) self-rising flour

¾ cup (175 g) superfine sugar

Finely grated zest of 2 lemons

1 tablespoon toasted poppy seeds

3 eggs

½ cup (125 ml) plain yogurt

½ cup (115 g) butter plus ¼ cup (60 g) Boosted Butter (page 12), melted

I

I Preheat the oven to 350°F (180°C/gas mark 4). Line a 12-cup muffin pan with paper baking cups. Mix the flour, sugar, lemon zest, and poppy seeds together in a mixing bowl.

2 Beat the eggs (man, those poor eggs are always in for a beating!) into the yogurt, then pour into the dry ingredients together and add the melted butter. Stir until just combined.

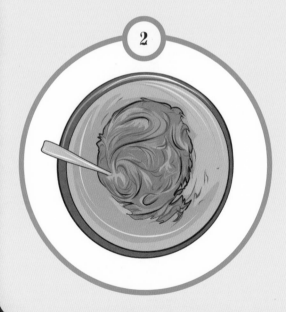

3 Spoon the batter into the pan and bake until a skewer inserted in the center comes out clean, 20–22 minutes. The cupcakes will be quite pale on top. Remove from the pan and place on a wire rack to cool completely. Then tuck in.

TAKE THE SKEWER TEST

It is important to test the muffins with a skewer as described, as the interior must be baked through before the muffins come out of the oven.

Lemon Cupcakes with Doobies

The Daily Rind

Fresh with the clean taste of lemon, these cupcakes are deliciously light, so long as you don't get any pith in there, and the little j's are adorable. Trust me, don't be tempted to use any spare lemons for fruit bongs—that's an eye-watering experience you'll never repeat.

Difficulty:
Easy

Makin' Time:
25 minutes

Bakin' Time:
20 minutes

Makes
12
cupcakes

1/4 cup (60 g) butter plus 1/4 cup (60 g) Boosted Butter (page 12)

1/2 cup (110 g) superfine sugar

2 eggs, beaten

1 cup (150 g) self-rising flour

Pinch of salt

Finely grated zest of 1 lemon

DOOBIES:

12 ounces (350 g) white decorator icing

3 thick vines black licorice

FROSTING:

2 cups (225 g) confectioners' sugar

3 tablespoons freshly squeezed lemon juice

1–2 teaspoons hot water

Yellow food coloring

ZEST IS BEST
When grating lemon zest, make sure you don't grate any of the white pith under the yellow skin, as this can be very bitter.

2 Gradually beat in the eggs, beating until fully blended. Gently stir in the flour, salt, and lemon zest until blended.

3

1

I Preheat the oven to 350°F (180°C/gas mark 4). Line a 12-cup muffin pan with paper baking cups. Beat the butter and sugar in a mixing bowl until pale and fluffy.

2

3 Spoon the batter into the prepared pan and bake until risen and springy to the touch, 15–20 minutes. Allow to cool in the pan for 5 minutes, then remove from the pan and place on a wire rack to cool completely. (You'll note this cooling process is always generally the same, but it bears repeating, cuz you're not known for your memory, are you?)

4 To make the doobies, roll out the decorator icing on nonstick baking paper. Cut each licorice stick into 3 pieces. Roll up each stick in a small amount of white decorator icing to resemble a doobie. Make a few extras so you can give one to your dopey buddy late one night and see if he tries to smoke it.

5 To make the frosting, sift the confectioners' sugar into a bowl and gradually stir in the lemon juice and just enough hot water until the mix is thick and smooth. Divide the frosting in half and color one half yellow.

6 Spread yellow frosting on half of the cupcakes and white frosting on the rest; smooth with a table knife or spatula. Place a doobie on each cupcake. Let set before serving.

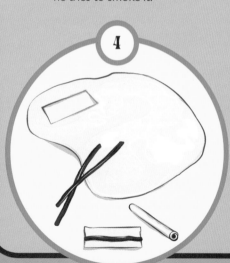

Juiced-Up Orange Muffins

Oh Yay to OJ

The humble orange, *Citrus sinensis* (or *Citrus sinsemilla*, as I prefer to call it) is the basis for this fruity taste explosion. Using the finely grated zest of the orange as well as its juice gives these muffins a real zing of flavor. Whichever way you look at it, they've got real a-peel!

Difficulty:
Easy

Makin' Time:
20 minutes

Bakin' Time:
25 minutes

2 1/2 tablespoons (35 g) butter plus
   2 1/2 tablespoons (35 g) Boosted Butter
   (page 12), melted

1 egg, beaten

3/4 cup (175 ml) plain yogurt

Juice and finely grated zest of 1 orange

2 1/4 cups (325g) all-purpose flour

1 tablespoon baking powder

2/3 cup (125 g) sugar

Makes
10
muffins

1 Preheat the oven to 350°F (180°C/gas mark 4). Line 10 cups of a 12-cup muffin pan with paper baking cups. Mix the butter, egg, yogurt, orange juice, and zest in a mixing bowl. Sift in the flour and baking powder and stir in the sugar.

2 Spoon the batter into the prepared pan and bake until risen and springy to the touch and golden, 20–25 minutes. Allow to cool in the pan for 5 minutes, then remove from the pan and place on a wire rack to cool completely. Two quick steps to success—now that's what I call nice 'n' easy baking for potheads.

ICE CREAM LOADUP
Chocolate and orange are a tried-and-true flavor combo: for a real treat, try serving these with some chocolate ice cream.

Apple Crisp Muffins

Green Day

If you love apple crisp, with its crunchy topping over tender baked apple chunks, you'll fall for these muffins. Obviously these little lovelies make a really tasty and unusual dessert when serving a meal to your friends. Enjoy with an apple bong.

Difficulty:
Easy

Makin' Time:
20 minutes

Bakin' Time:
20 minutes

TOPPING:

2 tablespoons butter

1 tablespoon all-purpose flour

2 tablespoons packed light brown sugar

2 tablespoons ground almonds

4 tablespoons sunflower seeds

MUFFINS:

2 cups (300 g) all-purpose flour

2 teaspoons baking powder

1/3 cup (80 g) packed light brown sugar

1 teaspoon mixed spices (cinnamon, nutmeg, ginger, cloves)

2 tart-sweet baking apples, peeled, cored, and chopped

1 egg

2/3 cup (150 ml) sour cream

1/4 cup (55 g) Boosted Butter (page 12), melted

Makes
12
muffins

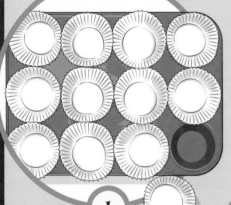

1 Preheat the oven to 375°F (190°C/gas mark 5). Line a 12-cup muffin pan with paper baking cups.

2 To make the topping, in a mixing bowl, cut the butter into the flour, sugar, and almonds until the mixture resembles breadcrumbs. Stir in the sunflower seeds and set aside.

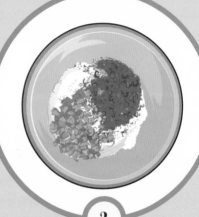

3 To make the muffins, sift the flour and baking powder into a mixing bowl. Stir in the sugar, mixed spices, and apple. In another bowl, mix together the egg, sour cream, and melted Boosted Butter.

4 Pour the wet ingredients into the dry and stir lightly until just combined. The mixture will be lumpy. (Nod if your diminished brain is following all this. Good.)

5 Spoon the batter into the muffin cups. Sprinkle the topping over the batter and bake until well risen and firm, 15–20 minutes. Allow to cool in the pan for a few minutes, then remove from the pan and place on a wire rack to cool completely.

APPLES 'N' LEMONS

Peel and chop the apples just before adding to the batter, to avoid browning from air exposure; you can also sprinkle them with a little freshly squeezed lemon juice and toss to coat.

chapter **5**

THE CHEF'S GONE NUTS

As if you're not nutty enough already, this chapter takes things further, with fresh, roasted, and ground pecans, peanuts, almonds, and more. As well as being pretty healthy (something your lifestyle is in dire need of), nuts are known to boost serotonin and endorphin levels. So, along with a generous dose of Mary Jane, these muffins and cupcakes will have you buzzing and smiling well into next week.

Almond Pirate Cupcakes

Jolly Roger

The marzipan, ground almonds, and almond extract give these cupcakes a truly memorable nutty flavor, while the topping will strike fear into any lily-livered land lubber. Rumor has it these were Blackbeard's favorite snack, but he always used to get the crumbs stuck in his whiskers.

Difficulty:
Medium

Makin' Time:
40 minutes

Bakin' Time:
25 minutes

8 ounces (225 g) marzipan, finely chopped

1 tablespoon (15 g) butter plus 1/4 cup (60 g) Boosted Butter (page 12)

1/2 cup (100 g) superfine sugar

3 eggs, beaten

1 tablespoon milk

3/4 cup (100 g) ground almonds

1 1/4 cups (175 g) all-purpose flour

2 teaspoons baking powder

1 teaspoon almond extract

FROSTING:

8 ounces (225 g) black decorator icing

3–4 tablespoons warmed apricot jelly

SKULLS AND CROSSBONES:

6 ounces (175 g) white decorator icing

Makes
12
cupcakes

2 Beat together the eggs and milk and gradually whisk the mixture into the paste, whisking constantly to make a smooth batter. Give your rolling hand a rest, then gently fold in the almonds, flour, baking powder, and almond extract until well blended.

1 Preheat the oven to 350°F (180°C/gas mark 4). Line a 12-cup muffin pan with paper baking cups. In a large, deep mixing bowl, beat the marzipan, Boosted Butter, and sugar to a smooth paste. Start with a fork and, once partly mixed, move on to an electric mixer.

3 Spoon the batter into the cupcake cups and bake until springy to the touch and golden, 20–25 minutes. Allow to cool in the pan for 5 minutes, then remove from the pan and place on a wire rack to cool completely.

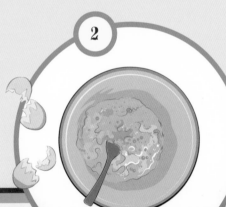

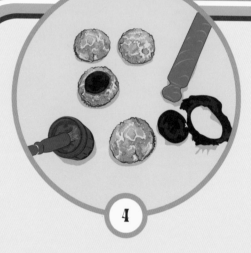

4

5 To make the skulls and crossbones, roll out the white decorator icing on a surface dusted with confectioners' sugar. Using a template as shown, cut out 12 skulls and crossbones. Lightly brush the cutouts with a little water and attach to the cupcakes. Arrrrr, me hearties!

MAN OVERBOARD
The skull-and-crossbones topping is fun, but if you prefer you can use the frosting on page 103 instead.

4 To make the frosting, roll out the black decorator icing on a surface lightly dusted with confectioners' sugar. Using a cookie cutter, cut out rounds the same size as the cupcakes. Brush the tops of the cupcakes with a little apricot jelly and attach the rounds.

5

Maple Pecan Cupcakes

Canadian Cook-Up

Makes
12
cupcakes

It's safe to say that just about all sweet-toothed stoners love the taste of maple syrup, and these cupcakes really deliver.

1/4 cup (60 g) butter plus 1/4 cup (60 g) Boosted Butter (page 12)

1/4 cup (55 g) packed light brown sugar

2/3 cup (150 ml) maple syrup

2 eggs

1 cup (150 g) self-rising flour

1/2 cup (55 g) chopped pecans

FROSTING AND DECORATION:

12 pecan halves

3 tablespoons butter

3 tablespoons maple syrup, plus extra for drizzling

1 1/4 cups (140 g) confectioners' sugar

Difficulty:
Medium

Makin' Time:
40 minutes

Bakin' Time:
25 minutes

ARE YOU SERIOUS—RIPE BRIE?

If you're a cheese lover, try the frosting with some pecan pieces spooned over some ripe Brie. You don't have to be French to love this.

1 Preheat the oven to 350°F (180°C/gas mark 4). Line a 12-cup muffin pan with paper baking cups. Beat the Boosted Butter and sugar together in a mixing bowl until creamy, then beat in the maple syrup.

2

3 Spoon the batter into the baking cups and bake until risen and golden, 15–20 minutes. Remove the pan from the oven but keep the heat on. Allow the cupcakes to cool in the pan for 5 minutes, then remove from the pan and place on a wire rack to cool completely.

1

2 Beat in the eggs, one at a time, until blended. Sift the flour into the mixture and gently stir until incorporated, then stir in the pecans.

3

5 In a mixing bowl, beat the butter and maple syrup until soft and creamy. Sift in the confectioners' sugar and beat until pale and fluffy, like little fluffy clouds, man.

4 While the cupcakes cool, make the frosting: put the pecan halves on a baking tray and put in the oven until they are lightly toasted, 5–6 minutes. (Now you can turn off the oven. Don't forget!) Set aside to cool.

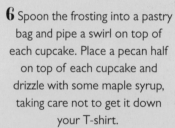

6 Spoon the frosting into a pastry bag and pipe a swirl on top of each cupcake. Place a pecan half on top of each cupcake and drizzle with some maple syrup, taking care not to get it down your T-shirt.

Coconut Cupcakes with Rolling Papers and Pot

Caribbean Smile

This lovely bunch of coconut cupcakes is a real tropical treat. The topping is enough to make you reach for your real rolling papers and stash—not that you need much encouragement. Or perhaps you might like to use a spare coconut as a novelty bong, instead? Decisions, decisions . . .

Difficulty:
Easy

Makin' Time:
20 minutes

Bakin' Time:
30 minutes

1/2 cup (115 g) butter plus 1/4 cup (60 g) Boosted Butter (page 12)

1 cup (225 g) superfine sugar

2 eggs

1 teaspoon vanilla extract

2 cups (300 g) all-purpose flour

2 teaspoons baking powder

1/2 cup (125 ml) plain yogurt

2 cups (175 g) flaked sweetened coconut

DECORATION:

12 ounces (350 g) white decorator icing

Confectioners' sugar, for dusting

4 tablespoons warmed apricot jelly

3 ice cream wafers or wafer cookies

1 cup (75 g) flaked sweetened coconut

Green food coloring

1 Preheat the oven to 350°F (180°C/gas mark 4). Line a 12-cup muffin pan with paper baking cups. Beat the Boosted Butter and sugar in a mixing bowl until light and fluffy. Gradually beat in the eggs and vanilla until smooth.

2

3 Spoon the batter into the baking cups (they'll pile quite high, but be sensible about it!) and bake until springy to the touch and golden, 25–30 minutes. Leave in the pans for 5 minutes, then remove from the pan and—guess what, folks?—place on a wire rack to cool completely.

2 Sift in the flour and baking powder, and gently fold into the mixture with the yogurt, until well combined. Stir in the coconut until blended.

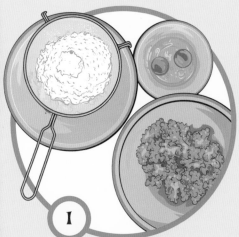

1

3

4 To decorate, roll out the decorator icing on a surface lightly dusted with confectioners' sugar. Using a cookie cutter, cut out 12 rounds the same size as the cupcakes. Brush the decorator icing rounds with a little apricot jelly and place carefully on the cupcakes, pressing lightly.

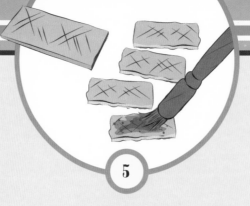

5

6 Put the coconut into a bowl and add a few drops of green coloring. Stir until evenly colored and sprinkle on top of the rolling papers.

5 Cut each wafer into 4 even-size rectangles as shown, and brush lightly with a little apricot jelly. Attach to the top of the cupcakes for the "rolling papers." *Now, does that look impressive or what?* No, not really, but it'll get you spaced just the same.

6

4

A TRULY SWEET HIGH

If you prefer a simpler topping, you can just add some more flaked sweetened coconut to a carton of whipped cream, together with some sugar and vanilla extract to taste, then spoon it onto the cupcakes.

Perfect Peanut Butter Muffins

Yummy in My Tummy

No one of sound or unsound mind can resist these muffins—they are just so moist and tasty. Even the unbaked batter is irresistible, so make sure you don't make too many PB&J sandwiches—you want to have some left to bake with.

Makes
12
muffins

Difficulty:
Easy

Makin' Time:
20 minutes

Bakin' Time:
25 minutes

2 1/2 cups (350 g) all-purpose flour

3/4 cup (150 g) sugar

1 tablespoon baking powder

Pinch of salt

2 eggs

3/4 cup (175 ml) milk

2 tablespoons sunflower oil, or other mild vegetable oil, such as canola

1/4 cup (60 g) Boosted Butter (page 12), melted

1/2 cup (110 g) smooth peanut butter

1 Preheat the oven to 350°F (180°C/gas mark 4). Line a 12-cup muffin pan with paper baking cups. Sift the flour, sugar, baking powder, and salt into a mixing bowl.

2

2 In another bowl (this'll probably need washing first—you'll find it in the sink with the remnants of last night's Ben & Jerry's), beat the eggs, milk, oil, butter, and peanut butter together until well combined. Stir into the dry ingredients until just mixed. The mixture should be slightly lumpy.

3 Spoon the batter into the muffin cups and bake until risen and golden, 20–25 minutes. Allow to cool in the pan for 5 minutes, then remove from the pan and place on a wire rack to cool completely, ready for munchie time.

1

3

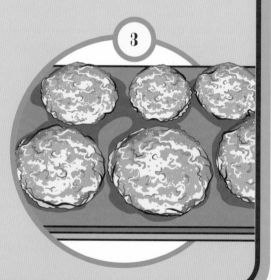

"Eyeball" Cupcakes

"You Lookin' at Me?"

Snickers fans and anyone with a really sweet tooth will love these. For some predictable childish humor, hold two decorated cupcakes up to your eyes and leap out on an unsuspecting family member.

Difficulty:
Easy

Makin' Time:
20 minutes

Bakin' Time:
20 minutes

Makes
12
cupcakes

2 3/4 cups (400 g) self-rising flour

1/2 cup (115 g) superfine sugar

1 cup (250 ml) buttermilk

1/2 cup (160 g) chocolate spread, such as Philadelphia or Whole Earth

1/4 cup (60 g) Boosted Butter (page 12), melted

1 egg

Two chocolate-caramel-nougat-peanut candy bars (such as Snickers), coarsely chopped

FROSTING:

2 cups (225 g) confectioners' sugar

1 teaspoon freshly squeezed lemon juice

2–3 tablespoons water

"EYEBALLS":

4 ounces (110 g) white decorator icing

24 blue and green chocolate jelly beans

Black icing gel

1 Preheat the oven to 400°F (200°C/gas mark 6). Grease a 12-cup muffin pan with a little butter. Sift the flour into a mixing bowl and stir in the sugar.

2 In another bowl, lightly whisk together the buttermilk, chocolate spread, Boosted Butter, and egg until just combined.

3 Stir the egg mixture into the flour mixture and mix until just combined. Do not overmix; it should still be a bit lumpy. Stir in the chopped candy bars and spoon the batter into the prepared pans. Don't eat all the candy bars or you'll have to start again.

DON'T OVERCUT THE CANDY

Don't cut the candy bars into pieces that are too small; you want identifiable traces of them left in the finished cupcakes. For a simpler topping, after frosting the cupcakes, just cut a third candy bar across into thin neat slices and put one on top of each cupcake.

5 To make the frosting, sift the confectioners' sugar into a bowl and gradually stir in the lemon juice and water until smooth and thick. Spread the frosting on the cupcakes.

4 Bake until a skewer (or joint poker) inserted into the centers comes out clean, about 20 minutes. Allow to cool in the pan for 5 minutes, then remove from the pan and place on a wire rack to cool completely.

6 To make the "eyeballs," roll out the decorator icing on a surface lightly dusted with confectioners' sugar. Using a suitable cutter (a donut hole cutter or a bottle top), cut out 24 small rounds for the eyes and place them on the frosted cupcakes. Brush the rounds with a little water and place a chocolate jelly bean in the center of each to form the "iris."

7 Pipe a tiny dab of black piping gel in the center of each bean for the "pupil." (Wiped out by the physiology lesson? Take a well-earned break to . . . recharge.)

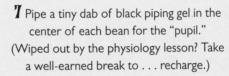

chapter **6**

PIMP THAT CUPCAKE!

It's time to up the ante with the Grand Prix of cupcake making. The ganja-themed toppings in this final chapter—from iconic artwork to Ken Kesey's Magic Bus—require a steady hand, so pack away your bong for a bit. These more complex decorations take more time and specialized equipment. Fear not! You can find items like shaped cutters in many specialty stores for the home cook, as well as on the Internet. Most of all, have fun!

"Pizza" Cupcakes

Stoned for Four Seasons

Next time you have a pizza-and-a-movie night—watching the Cheech and Chong back catalog—try these for dessert. They take a while to make, but are well worth it, cuz if the movie marathon don't make you go crosseyed, then the active ingredient sure will!

Makes
12
cupcakes

Difficulty:
Medium

Makin' Time:
30 minutes

Bakin' Time:
20 minutes

1 3/4 cups (250 g) all-purpose flour

2 1/2 teaspoons baking powder

1/2 cup (110 g) sugar

1/2 teaspoon salt

3/4 cup (180 ml) milk

3 tablespoons sunflower oil plus 3 tablespoons Souped-Up Sunflower Oil (page 15)

1 egg

3/4 cup (175 g) chopped macadamia nuts

FROSTING:

1 1/4 cups (150 g) confectioners' sugar

4–5 teaspoons hot water

Red food coloring

DECORATION:

3 ounces (75 g) white chocolate

4 ounces (110 g) brown decorator icing

2 ounces (55 g) green decorator icing

1 Preheat the oven to 400°F (200°C/gas mark 6). Grease a 12-cup muffin pan with a little butter. Mix the flour, baking powder, sugar, and salt in a mixing bowl.

2 In a small bowl, mix the milk, oil, and egg. Stir into the dry ingredients along with the nuts. Stir until just combined. The mixture will be lumpy.

3 Spoon the batter into the prepared pan and bake until golden brown and risen, about 20 minutes. Allow to cool in the pan for 5 minutes, then remove from the pan and place on a wire rack to cool completely.

4

4 Slice the tops off the cupcakes as evenly as possible; reserve the tops for the finishing presentation of the cupcakes—or you can just eat them as chef's treats!

5 To make the frosting, sift the confectioners' sugar into a bowl and gradually stir in the water and a few drops of red food coloring; you want a rich tomato-sauce effect. Spread the frosting over the newly flat tops of the cupcakes.

5

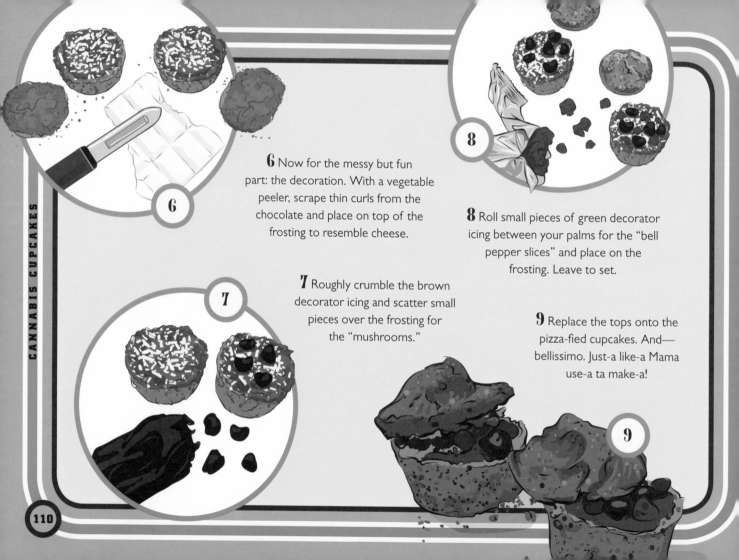

6 Now for the messy but fun part: the decoration. With a vegetable peeler, scrape thin curls from the chocolate and place on top of the frosting to resemble cheese.

7 Roughly crumble the brown decorator icing and scatter small pieces over the frosting for the "mushrooms."

8 Roll small pieces of green decorator icing between your palms for the "bell pepper slices" and place on the frosting. Leave to set.

9 Replace the tops onto the pizza-fied cupcakes. And—bellissimo. Just-a like-a Mama use-a ta make-a!

Quarter Pounders

Mister Mac's Wicked Cousin

Sweet tooth or not, any food lover will "relish" these cupcake burgers. You can have plenty of fun making your own fixins' from colored icing—ketchup, mustard, bacon, cheese, red onion, the works! Ronald McDonald eat your heart out.

Difficulty:
Medium

Makin' Time:
40 minutes

Bakin' Time:
30 minutes

"BURGER BUNS":

1/2 cup (125 g) butter

1 cup (200 g) superfine sugar

1 large egg, beaten

3 cups (450 g) all-purpose flour

1 teaspoon baking soda

1/2 teaspoon salt

1 1/4 cups (300 ml) buttermilk

CHOCOLATE CAKE "BURGERS":

1/8 cup (15 g) cocoa powder

1 1/4 cups (175 g) all-purpose flour

1/2 teaspoon baking soda

1/2 teaspoon baking powder

Pinch of salt

2 tablespoons (30 g) butter plus 2 tablespoons (30 g) Boosted Butter (page 12)

1/3 cup (75 g) packed dark brown sugar

1/2 egg, beaten

1/4 cup (60 ml) milk

1/2 teaspoon vanilla extract

FILLING:

1 cup (200 g) hazelnut chocolate spread, such as Nutella

DECORATION:

1 cup (100 g) confectioners' sugar

Water

Red food coloring

Yellow food coloring

6 ounces (175 g) green decorator icing

Makes
6
"burgers"

1 Finish your drive-through meal and get ready to work. Preheat the oven to 350°F (180°C/gas mark 4). Line 3 large cookie sheets with nonstick baking paper.

2 To make the "buns," beat the butter and sugar in a mixing bowl until light and fluffy. Gradually beat in the egg until blended. Sift in the flour, baking soda, and salt and gently stir in until incorporated. Stir in the buttermilk in increments until the batter is smooth and thick—you may not need all of it. (Drink any that's left over. Yum!)

3 Drop 2-tablespoon scoops of the mixture onto the cookie sheets, about 2 inches (4 cm) apart, 4 to a sheet.

4 Bake until a skewer inserted into the center comes out clean, 10–15 minutes. Allow to cool in the pan for a few minutes, then remove from the pan and place on a wire rack to cool completely.

5 To make the burgers, reduce the oven temperature to 325°F (160°C/gas mark 3) and add fresh paper linings to the cookie sheets. Sift together the cocoa, flour, baking soda, baking powder, and salt into a large mixing bowl. Mix well (and do try to keep most of it in the bowl).

6 In another bowl, beat together the Boosted Butter, sugar, and egg until smooth and light. In a third bowl (I hope you've got enough bowls; you'll probably find a few dirty ones in the sink), lightly beat together the milk and vanilla extract.

7

9

8 Bake until firm to the touch, about 15 minutes. Allow to cool in the pan for a few minutes, then remove from the pan and place on a wire rack to cool completely.

9 Keep your concentration: it's time to assemble the burgers. Spread half of the plain cake rounds with hazelnut chocolate spread. That's the bottom half of the bun.

7 Add alternating thirds of the dry cocoa mixture and the milk mixture to the egg mixture, beating until smooth. Spoon the batter into 6 rounds on the relined cookie sheets, keeping them about 2 inches (5 cm) apart.

6

10 Place a chocolate cake round on top (that's your burger) and spread lightly with chocolate spread.

11 To make the decoration, sift the confectioners' sugar into a bowl. Stir in just enough water to make a thick, smooth frosting. Put half the frosting into another bowl.

12 Color one bowl of frosting red and the other yellow to resemble ketchup and mustard. Drizzle over the burgers, allowing it to run down the sides just like real condiments. Hey, this looks good enough to eat! Which is handy, cuz that's what you'll be doing soon.

13 Roll out the green decorator icing and cut or tear into thin strips to resemble lettuce leaves.

14 Place the leaves on the edges of the burgers and top with the remaining plain cakes—the tops of the buns, of course. Open wide!

Screamin' Ginger Cupcakes

They're a Nightmare

This freaky cupcake is based on the famous painting *The Scream* by Norwegian artist Edvard Munch, which dates from 1893 and is still pretty haunting today—especially if you happen to be trippin' on some cerebral sativa. It certainly weirded-out old Edvard; he hit the bottle and claimed he was "verging on madness" by 1908. So don't eat too many!

Difficulty:
Difficult, but so worth it

Makin' Time:
1 hour

Bakin' Time:
25 minutes

Makes 12 cupcakes

2 1/4 cups (325 g) all-purpose flour

1 cup (200 g) packed light brown sugar

2 teaspoons baking powder

3 teaspoons ground ginger

1 teaspoon pumpkin pie spice

1/4 teaspoon grated nutmeg

Pinch of ground cloves

2 eggs

7 tablespoons clear honey

1/4 cup (60 g) butter plus 1/4 cup (60 g) Boosted Butter (page 12), melted

3/4 cup (175 ml) hot water

2 tablespoons chopped candied ginger

DECORATION:

12 ounces (350 g) white decorator icing

Confectioners' sugar, for dusting

Icing gel colors: pink, chestnut, dark brown, eggplant/purple, melon/orange, copper/flesh, navy blue, sky blue

2–3 tablespoons apricot jelly, warmed

1 Preheat the oven to 350°F (180°C/gas mark 4). Line a 12-cup muffin pan with paper baking cups. Sift the flour, sugar, baking powder, and spices into a mixing bowl.

2 In another bowl, beat together the eggs, honey, and Boosted Butter until smooth. Stir into the dry ingredients. Add the water and chopped ginger and stir well until combined.

3 Spoon the batter into the muffin cups and bake until they are golden and a skewer inserted into the center comes out clean, 20–25 minutes. Allow to cool in the pan for 10 minutes, then remove from the pan and place on a wire rack to cool completely. Take a spliff break and then steady your nerves for the terrifying topping.

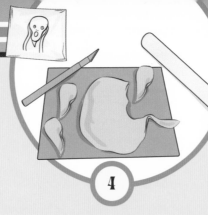

4

4 To make the decoration, roll out the white decorator icing to about the thickness of a nickel, $1/16$ inch (2 mm), on a surface lightly dusted with confectioner's sugar. Using a template, cut out 12 long "Scream" heads from the paste. Don't wimp out now.

5 Paint faces on these heads, using copper/flesh color icing gel for the skin; chestnut, dark brown, and eggplant/purple for the eyebrows and to outline the chin; and a touch of melon/orange on the cheeks. Let dry, and smoke a bowl.

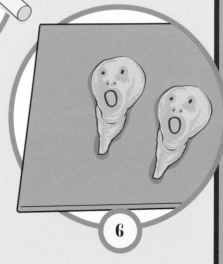

6

6 Once the faces are dry, using a fine brush and navy blue color, add the mouth, nose, and eyes. Whoa, it's looking pretty realistic now.

7 Using a cookie cutter, cut out 12 rounds the size of the cupcakes from the remaining white decorator icing.

8 Brush these rounds on one side with warm apricot jelly and carefully place them on top of the cupcakes. You may need to shave a little off the top of the cupcakes to get the rounds to lie smoothly.

9 Paint in the background sky, using navy, sky blue, chestnut, dark brown, and eggplant/purple. Leave to dry. Time for a quick joint.

10 Once the paint is dry, gently brush the underside of the little portraits with water and position them on the tops of the cakes.

11 Roll some fondant into thin ropes and cut them into 24 1/4-inch (5 mm) lengths. Shape these into arms with narrow hands at one end, and place them alongside the face to complete the picture.

11

12 Paint the figures' arms and hands with copper/flesh and some brown, and the screamer's shirt with navy. Leave all this to dry. Agghh!! Run to Mommy now!

12

9

Om Lotus Honey Cupcakes

Hindu Highs

The Om symbol is central to both Hinduism and Buddhism, and the vibrating mantra it represents is said to be the sound of the universe. But you don't have to be the Dalai Lama to get something out of it. These cupcakes are challenging to make, and once baking is over you'll be ready for a meditative Om session. So clear your chakras, listen to the sounds of the waves . . . and prepare to get seriously smashed!

Difficulty:
Difficult

Makin' Time:
50 minutes

Bakin' Time:
20 minutes

1/2 cup (115 g) butter plus 1/6 cup (45 g) Boosted Butter (page 12)

4 tablespoons clear honey

6 tablespoons milk

1 egg

2/3 cup (100 g) all-purpose flour

1 1/2 teaspoons baking powder

1/2 teaspoon baking soda

1 teaspoon pumpkin pie spice

2 teaspoons ground cinnamon

1 apple

DECORATION:

14 ounces (400 g) pink decorator icing

Confectioners' sugar, for dusting

3 tablespoons apricot jelly, warmed

4 ounces (115 g) white decorator icing

Red royal or cookie icing

1 Preheat the oven to 350°F (180°C/gas mark 4). Line 8 cups of a 12-cup muffin pan with paper baking cups. Beat together the butter and honey in a mixing bowl until smooth. Beat in the milk and egg until well incorporated.

2 Sift in the flour, baking powder, baking soda, spice, and ground cinnamon and gently stir everything together. The batter will of course be lumpy, but that's cool. Peel and chop the apple, and stir in.

3 Spoon into the muffin cups and bake until a skewer or wooden cocktail stick inserted into the center comes out clean, 15–20 minutes. Allow to cool in the pan for 5 minutes, then remove from the pan and place on a wire rack to cool completely. (Cooler than a Coors Light? Not quite that cool.)

4 To make the decoration, on a surface lightly dusted with confectioners' sugar roll out half the pink decorator icing to the thickness of a nickel, about 1/16 inch (2 mm). Using a petunia-shaped cutter or something similar, cut out 8 flower shapes. (Ah, so sweet and pretty.) Using a modeling tool or spoon handle, score a line or two down the middle of each petal on each shape as shown.

5

4

5 Place each flower shape upside-down on a small upturned cup or bowl to shape it into a curve, and leave them to dry slightly; they should still be pliable.

6 Roll out half the remaining pink decorator icing, slightly thinner than before. Using a suitable cookie cutter, cut out 8 rounds the size of the cupcakes and set aside.

7 Roll out the rest of the pink decorator icing to the same thickness and cut out 8 small petals per cupcake, using a spade cutter or any suitable petal cutter. Score a vein in the middle of each as for the larger petals (keeping well away from your own veins).

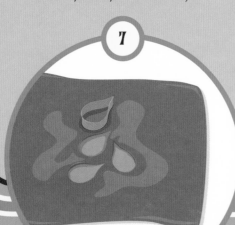

8 Brush the top of each cupcake with warm apricot jelly and position the petals around the cupcake so that the petals hang over the rim. You may need to shave a little off the top of the cupcakes to get the petals to lie smoothly. Cover the petals with the icing rounds to hold them in position.

9 To make the "Om" sign, roll out the white decorator icing to the thickness of a nickel, about 1/16 inch (2 mm) and, using a rose petal cutter, cut out 8 petals. (Are you following all this?) Lay them out in a row, pointed side up.

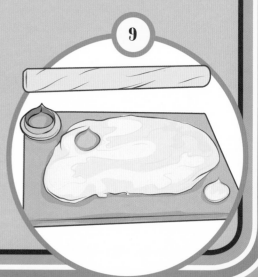

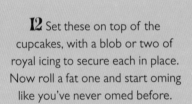

II To assemble the decoration, place a blob of royal icing in the middle of the curved flower shape, then position an "Om" symbol petal upright on it, and leave it to dry.

I2 Set these on top of the cupcakes, with a blob or two of royal icing to secure each in place. Now roll a fat one and start oming like you've never omed before.

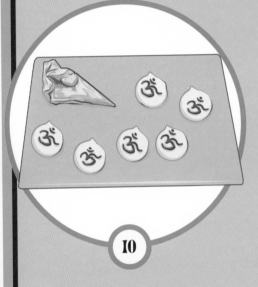

IO

IO Using red royal icing and a number 2 piping nozzle, pipe a red "Om" symbol on each petal and leave to dry. Om quietly to them if you like.

Magic Bus Red Velvet Cupcakes

Makes 12 cupcakes

The Road to Nowhere

Ken Kesey's wildly painted school bus, in which he and his band of Merry Pranksters made their LSD-fueled journey across America "in search of a kool place," has since been mythologized as the vehicle that launched the psychedelic '60s. This evocation of it in icing would make the perfect way to say bon voyage to those embarking on a similar adventure.

Difficulty:
Difficult

Makin' Time:
50 minutes

Bakin' Time:
20 minutes

1 1/4 cups (175 g) self-rising flour

2 tablespoons cocoa powder

1/2 teaspoon baking soda

Pinch of salt

7 tablespoons buttermilk

1 teaspoon white vinegar

1/2 teaspoon vanilla extract

1 tablespoon red food coloring

1/4 cup (60 g) Boosted Butter (page 12)

3/4 cup (175 g) superfine sugar

1 egg

DECORATION:

8 ounces (225 g) white decorator icing

Confectioners' sugar, for dusting

Icing gel colors: red, yellow, eggplant/ purple, and navy blue

1 ounce (30 g) black decorator icing

Edible silver food dust

12 ounces (375 g) green decorator icing

3 tablespoons white royal icing

3 tablespoons warmed apricot jelly

1 Preheat the oven to 325°F (160°C/gas mark 3). Line a 12-cup muffin pan with paper baking cups. Stir together the flour, cocoa, baking soda, and salt in a mixing bowl. In another bowl, mix the buttermilk, vinegar, vanilla, and red food coloring.

2 In another, large mixing bowl (check the sink again—wash one if you must), beat the Boosted Butter and sugar together until light and fluffy. Beat in the egg a little at a time. Mix in one-third of the flour mixture, followed by half of the buttermilk mixture, then another third of the flour, the remaining buttermilk, and finally the last of the flour mixture.

3 Spoon the batter into the baking cups and bake until risen and golden, about 20 minutes. Allow to cool in the pan for 5 minutes, then remove from the pan and place on a wire rack to cool completely.

4 To make the decoration, on a surface lightly dusted with confectioners' sugar, roll out the white decorator icing to the thickness of a nickel, about 1/16 inch (2 mm). Using a template, cut out 12 magic bus shapes. ("Too much, the magic bus!")

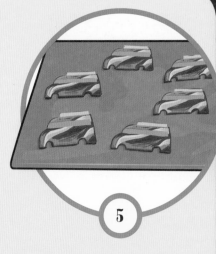

5

5. Now get creative. Use icing gel to paint the buses with stripes of red, yellow, eggplant/purple, and blue. Leave to dry.

4

6 Using the black decorator icing, roll out a sausage shape to 1/3 inch (3/4 cm) thick, and cut across it to make 24 disks. Roll each disk into a ball and gently press down to make a wheel. Using a star nozzle, impress a wheel cap in the middle of each wheel. Using a dry paint brush, brush the middle of each wheel with silver powder to make a hubcap. Stick the wheels to the buses using dabs of water. (Don't make the mistake I did and get this black decorator icing mixed up with your sticky Afghan hash.)

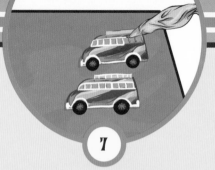

7 Using piping nozzle number 1.5 and the white royal icing, pipe in the windows and lights and the carrier at the top of each bus. Leave to dry. Brush silver powder on the piping, over the windows and the carrier on top of the bus. Paint the headlights yellow. (Art was never this much fun in eighth grade.)

8 On a surface lightly dusted with confectioners' sugar, roll out the green decorator icing to the thickness of a nickel, about 1/16 inch (2 mm). Using a cookie cutter the size of the cupcakes, cut out 12 rounds.

9 Using yellow icing gel, paint a starburst on each round of green decorator icing, starting from the middle. Gently brush the back of the dried green rounds with warm apricot jelly and place on the cupcakes. You may have to shave the top to make a flat surface.

10 Brush the back of the buses with a wet brush and place one on the middle of each cupcake top. Let the trip commence.

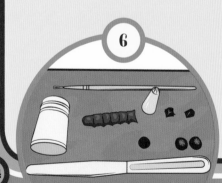

124

Spicy Rasta Cupcakes

Ragga Trip

What could be more fun for an honorary Rastafarian like yourself than a cupcake that evokes a dreadlocked Rasta wearing an iconic multicolored rastacap? These will be a hit at any party where you want people to let their hair down. Offer your praises to Jah before you tuck in, and when you open your eyes (three hours later), you'll be in Zion.

Difficulty:
Difficult

Makin' Time:
50 minutes

Bakin' Time:
25 minutes

2 cups (300 g) all-purpose flour

2 teaspoons baking powder

1/2 teaspoon baking soda

1 teaspoon ground cinnamon

1/2 teaspoon ground ginger

1/2 teaspoon pumpkin pie spice

1/2 teaspoon salt

1 can (15–16 ounces/ 425–450 g) pumpkin purée

3 tablespoons (45 g) butter plus 3 tablespoons (45 g) Boosted Butter (page 12), melted

1/2 cup (120 ml) evaporated milk

1/2 cup (110 g) packed light brown sugar

1/4 cup (55 g) sugar

2 large eggs, beaten

1 teaspoon vanilla extract

1/2 cup (75 g) raisins

DECORATION:

8 ounces (225 g) brown decorator icing

Confectioners' sugar, for dusting

3 tablespoons apricot jelly, warmed

8 ounces (225 g) green decorator icing

2 ounces (50 g) yellow decorator icing

2 ounces (50 g) red decorator icing

6 ounces (175 g) black decorator icing

PIMP THAT CUPCAKE!

1 Preheat the oven to 375°F (190°C/ gas mark 5). Line a 12-cup muffin pan with paper baking cups. Sift the flour, baking powder, baking soda, spices, and salt into a mixing bowl.

2 Whisk together the pumpkin purée, melted butter, evaporated milk, both sugars, eggs, and vanilla until blended. Stir the wet mixture into the dry ingredients until just combined. Gently stir in the rabbit poo (sorry, raisins—it doesn't look too great at the moment, but bear with it).

NO PUMPKIN, NO CRY
If you haven't got any pumpkin purée, then any fruit-based purée will do.

3 Spoon the batter into the cupcake cups and bake until risen and golden, 20–25 minutes. Allow to cool in the pan for 5 minutes, then remove from the pan and place on a wire rack to cool completely. Feelin' irie, man.

4 To make the decoration, roll out the brown decorator icing on a surface lightly dusted with confectioners' sugar. Using a cookie cutter the size of the cupcake, cut out 12 rounds. Lightly brush the rounds with warm apricot jelly and place one on each cupcake. You may need to shave the tops of the cupcakes flat to get the rounds to lie smoothly.

5 Roll out the green decorator icing to the thickness of 1 1/2 nickels, about 1/10 inch (3 mm), and cut out 12 rounds 1 1/2 inches (4 cm) in diameter to form the rasta caps. Okay, now we're jammin'.

6 Roll out the yellow decorator icing to the thickness of a nickel, 1/16 inch (1.5 mm), and cut out 12 strips 1/4 inch (7 mm) wide and 4 3/4 inches (12 cm) long, and stick each to the edge of a green cap with a little water. Set the caps aside.

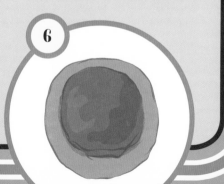

6

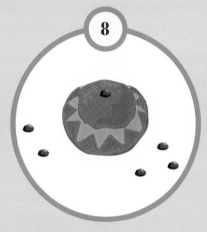

7 Roll out the red decorator icing to about half the thickness of a nickel, 1/24 inch (1 mm) and cut out 12 strips 1/5 inch (5 mm) wide and 4 3/4 inches (12 cm) long. (Yes, that is a very narrow strip.) Then cut a zigzag edge down one side of each. (Man, this is hard.) Stick each down on each of the yellow strips with a little water.

8 Gently press a knitted fabric or a sieve onto the whole piece to achieve the knitted look. Roll very small amounts of black decorator icing into little balls and place on the cap.

9 Using the remaining black decorator icing, make dreadlocks by rolling out thin snakes, cutting into various lengths (you'll need 72 in total) and tapering the ends.

10 Dab the undersides of the caps lightly with a wet brush and place them on top of the dreadlocks. Look, it's Pete Tosh!